Drumming Up Referrals

Dan Bodanis

The Referral Press Inc.

Published by Referral Press Inc.
First Edition, August 2000
Second Edition, October 2003

ISBN 0-9685005-01

Business Trade Book

Cover Design: Central Reproductions Ltd.
Cover Photos: Ron Eckroth, Studio 51 Photography
Book Design: Lar deSouza
Typesetting: Central Reproductions Ltd.
4524 Eastgate Parkway
Mississauga ON L4W 3W6
Contact Person: Doug Snow, Vice-President
Dave Anderson, Customer Service

Printed in Canada

DEDICATIONS

This book is dedicated
to my family.

My wife, Kelly

My father and mother,
Tom & Elen Bodanis

My sister,
Cyndi Bodanis

My in-laws,
Adolf & Claudette Schrempf

My brother and sister-in-law,
Gary and Christy Schrempf

My nephew,
Benjamin Schrempf

You are always there.

CONTENTS

THE PEOPLE WHO HELPED MAKE THIS BOOK POSSIBLE

This book was brought to life through the coordinated, tireless, selfless, dedicated efforts of many people. These people gave their time, energy and intellect in helping to get the important messages it contains into your hands.

These people booked me to speak at meetings. They gave me positive suggestions for improvement, they inspired me and they believed in me right from the start.

With great pride, I call these people my Teachers, Colleagues, Mentors, Mastermind Partners, Family, and most importantly, I call these people my Friends.

Throughout my life, I have been blessed with friendships that have helped shape my destiny in the most positive way imaginable.

To celebrate the enormous contribution this esteemed group has made to myself and ultimately to you, the reader, I would like to formally acknowledge them.

The only thing better than getting to know their names, so as to watch for their stars as they rise, is getting to know them in person. They are:

Murray & Geri Ross
Tim Plaxton
Don Faso
David Roth
Bill Roth
John Mazziotti
David Schwartz
Jeremy Parsons
David Cuthbertson
Paul Jennings
Blair Fraser
Bill Evans
Mary Lennox
David Cowper

Leanne Simons
Andy Buckstein
Earl Hunter
David Parsons
Garth Coleman
Toney Philadelphia
Dan Scepanovic
David Harvey
Pat Reith
Gerry Hyde
Bud Platts
Cindy Grant
Wayne Blanchard
Dave Rundell
Bill Charles
Mark Stacey
Bob Mizak
Lee Loveridge
Paula Kidd
Sanjay Mehrota
Brian Schreyer
Tom Van Tigham
Stewart Mulder
Paul & Sandy McKay
Tom McInerney
Kevin Sampson
Paul Karasik
Terry Farrell
John Faiola
Rob Ferguson
Gwen Borins
Jimmy Bazos
Tim Whelan
Darren Coleman
Pat Tauskela
Mike Croucher
Derek Balmer
Steve Goebels
Doug Dawson
Arthur Preto
Duson Novak
Gary Gradley
Peter Stairs
Brian Mennis
Perry Catena
Brian Hind
Jon Morrison
Gerry Legge
Ruth Lorayes
Terry Basaraba
Doug Bray
Floyd Black
Vas Pachapurcar
Ken Zukiwski
Doug McLeish
Bob Nuttall
Dr. Uma Prasada
Sylvia Henderson
Paul Bates

Wayne Cadugan
Dr. Patrick F. Hewitt
Bruce Shriver
Anna Kubicek
Gilles Marceau
Leo Belmonte
Cliff Oliver
Geoff Elliott
Marion Illiohan
Juan & John Sanchez
Gord Lemon & Kelita Haverland-Lemon
Esther Bast
Dr. Mark Fleet
Rex Eveliegh
Eileen Madder
Al Gallo
Bala Naidoo
Steve Carlson
François Fillion
Marc Atkinson

OF SPECIAL NOTE

Exceptional people, great products, and outstanding services! Here are a few of the people, products and services that you must get to know and do business with. In giving these referrals, I offer you my heartfelt endorsement and sincerely believe you will benefit beyond expectation.

Besides, what credibility would a book like this have, if it didn't provide you with a few great referrals?

Boofy Biscotti's, Great Gourmet Biscotti's, Kelly Bodanis 416-720-7164
Central Reproductions, Total Print Management (Printing and much more!)
Doug Snow 905-238-1250

Wine Consultant

Global Beverage Concepts, Susie Chen, President Susie.gbc@sympatico.ca

Restaurants

Summit Garden Chinese Restaurant, Ken Choi or Lawrence Lo
Mississauga, www.summitgarden.com 905-828-6686
Ravenous Catering, Jason Pilkington, 13 East Mill St., 519-846-8738
Elora, Ontario
Izzy's Restaurant, Izzy Kobylanski, 905-521-1503
354 Main St West, Hamilton, Ontario
Richview Bakery & Deli, Mario Stellato, Etobicoke 416-248-4662
Georgio's Ristorante (formerly Cinque) Italian Cuisine, Georgio Albiati
Mississauga 905-826-9291
Antonelli's Italian Ristorante, 200 County Court Blvd
and Hurontario, Brampton 905-450-5322
Rogues Restaurant, 1900 Dundas St. Mississauga 905-822-2670

Oliver Bonacini Restaurants: (Toronto)
Canoe, 66 Wellington St West 54th floor,
Toronto Dominion Bank Tower 416-364-0054
Biff's, 4 Front St. 416-860-0086
Jump, Commerce Court East,
Wellington St., West side of Yonge St. 416-363-3400
Auberge du Pomier, 4150 Yonge St. 416-222-2220

referrals continued on page 180

INTRODUCTION:

THE RHYTHM OF SUCCESS

DRUM: TO SUMMON BY OR AS BY THE BEAT OF A DRUM; . . .TO OBTAIN (CUSTOM, CUSTOMERS) BY CANVASSING OR SOLICITATIONS .

Oxford English Dictionary

Who sets the beat that will march you to success? The beat drummed out by entrepreneurs and sales professionals not only sets the measure of their working lives. It calls out to clients and customers. Drummers do not chase business; they attract it.

Why do you need to drum up more business? Maybe there's a sailboat with your name on it, a condo high overlooking the city or a beachfront property with sunsets to die for. Close your eyes for a moment: Watch your children graduate from university; Hear your name called out at Awards Night; Burn your mortgage or pay off your credit cards.

You know what success feels like. You can hear the crack of the golf club as it connects. You can watch the shot rebound into the net. You can feel the firm handshake of the satisfied client. Not only are you calling the tune, you're setting the beat that keeps everyone together. Competent, confident, collected: in success, you are ready to deal with problems and turn them into new achievements.

The 'drumming' lessons in this book will show you how to set a beat that summons all the new business you want. You don't need a drum or even a sense of rhythm. If you believe that you can succeed, you can learn to drum up new business. When one client marches to your beat, you are one step closer to success. When a parade of clients march to your beat, you have success.

The key to success is not in the business you have now, but in the four letter word: **N E X T**. Where will your next customer or client come from? The **N E X T** client is the one who makes today's business grow again tomorrow. When you are sure that you have customers lined up into the future, you can also be sure of success.

This is why so many businesses spend enormous amounts of money and effort to line up their **NEXT** clients. Advertising, special events, public relations and even cold calling are all ways to look for new clients. They all cost money that takes away from your bottom line. They almost all require you to enter into activities that are beyond your normal comfort zone.

Only one path promises to take you directly from today's deals to tomorrow's sales: referrals. When a client gives you a referral, he or she is giving you your **NEXT** customer. This allows you to concentrate on providing the best possible goods and service. It frees up the time, energy, and money you would otherwise have to spend looking for new business. Referrals take you from where you are to where your next customer waits for you presold on the value and service that you represent.

Referrals may range from a personal introduction to a phone number written on the back of a business card. Essentially, however, all referrals are a form of introduction in which your current clients recommend that you do business with their friends, relatives, customers, or colleagues. Whether your client offers you a list of names and phone numbers or speaks to potential customers on your behalf, a referral says: "I have already tested the waters and found that this product or service represents good value. I believe that you, too, would benefit from listening to what this professional has to say." When you speak with a referred prospect, you have the wind in your sails long before you launch into a sales presentation.

Your meeting with a referred client is only the beginning. Each client who is referred to you is also a potential source of more referrals. Every customer you contact, even those who decide not to do business with you, can (and might) give you referrals. Only one question stands between you and unlimited success. If ***you can ask*** for a referral, you can line up your **NEXT** client while concluding business.

When you ask a client for a referral, you begin your **NEXT** client contact before the original sale is over. You never have to wonder where you will find your next client, or spend hours devising complicated and expensive marketing plans. Instead of cold-calling, you may find that prospects are now calling you.

In fact, there is no question that referrals are the best possible way to build your business. They are inexpensive and effective. Your success can be built on referrals if you are willing to ask for them, ready to follow-up on them, and committed to giving your best to every potential client. When you are fully prepared to make the most out of every chance to get referrals, you are fully prepared for success.

DRUMMING UP REFERRALS will help you to explore the process that puts the **NEXT** client within easy reach of your phone. Together, we will look at what makes you referable and why your clients will be happy to become your most valuable source of new business. Then

DRUMMING UP REFERRALS will provide you with the tools you need to ask for - and get - more referrals, today, tomorrow, forever. You will learn what to say when you ask for referrals, how you should say it, and even how you should work up enough nerve to put your new skills to use.

I realize that one of the reasons you are reading this book is probably that you would rather read than ask for referrals. I know that virtually everyone dreads the moment in a sales appointment when it becomes time to ask for referrals. But I also know that anyone who reads this entire book and makes an honest effort will be rewarded with many new referrals and exciting growth in business. If you do as I say, I guarantee that you will drum up more referrals.

How do I know the techniques I describe are sure to work for you? First of all, I know because I have tried them myself. Second, I know because many of my scripts and approaches have been shared with me by people who are at the very top of their professions. Finally, I know because I have given seminars to thousands of people, many of whom have achieved extraordinary results with the techniques they learned from me.

LEARNING TO ASK FOR REFERRALS

Like me, you were probably not born with an innate talent for getting referrals. Few of us are blessed with an almost magical ability to persuade clients to offer us the names and phone numbers of their friends and acquaintances. Instead, most of us find that our early efforts to ask for referrals run smack into a wall of objections.

When I became a financial planner, I quickly lost any illusions about referrals falling naturally into my hands. My 'natural market' of friends and acquaintances saw me only as a "drummer." They did not want to do business with me, and they did not want to recommend that others do business with me. I began to panic!

With fear nipping at my heels, I turned to my mentor, Gabor Szekely.

When Gabor began his career in financial planning, he had no natural market. All his friends and associates were in Hungary; Gabor was in Canada. And yet, within a few short years, Gabor went from selling paintings from the back of his Volkswagen Beetle to extraordinary success as a financial planner. Along the way, Gabor was a fine drummer, and my drum teacher.

When I told Gabor that my own natural market was drying up, he did not question me about marketing or cold-calling. He asked how I was trying to get referrals. I told him that I had a sheet I handed clients at the end of an appointment. It had spaces for the names of six people who would benefit from financial planning. Occasionally, a client would actually fill in a few names. More often, I heard: "let me think about it. I want to see some benefits before I give you the names of my friends" or "Let me have my friends call you." No one called.

Gabor suggested that I needed to find a better approach. He told me one way that worked well for him. He would ask his clients, "Do you know anyone who would like to benefit from my 10 years of experience?"

"Great," I said to Gabor. "But what am I supposed to ask? Do you know anyone who would benefit from my 10 minutes of experience?"

My problem at that time was not unusual for a young professional. How could I hope for referrals before I had spent enough time in my profession to provide extraordinary customer service to anybody? Would it be possible to increase my referral base even if no opportunities for unusual rapport presented themselves? Why would someone make a referral when I had not yet proven myself? Have you ever asked yourself these questions?

Instead of giving up and going back to playing the drums in night-clubs, I decided to do some research. In a rare moment of absolute clarity, I knew that whatever time I spent thinking about how to attract good referrals would pay huge dividends. I spent every second of available time creating and practicing ways to ask for referrals. By approaching the problem systematically, I learned how and when to ask for referrals. As a result, the referrals began flowing in! Soon, I actually had a list of people who were waiting to see me.

Some of these referred clients replaced those I annoyed while learning. Once, I pushed so hard for a referral that I provoked a client to scream, "All you care about is referrals. Referrals, referrals, referrals!" Memories like this remind me never to rely on my natural charm to produce referrals. The success I have since achieved has not resulted from great natural talent. I have made the most of my natural abilities by working through the skills and strategies that lead to success.

I **LEARNED** how to ask for referrals (and how not to ask) by studying the techniques of the most successful people I knew. I **LEARNED** how to be more sensitive to the needs and goals of my clients. I **LEARNED** how to overcome my own ***doubts and fears***. And I know you can **LEARN** these things, too.

EARNING YOUR REFERRALS

My personal experience has proven to me that anyone can drum up more referrals. simply by asking for them. The people who get the most referrals, however, have one extra secret. They all believe that it is essential to "treat people in the best way possible." They combine excellent skills with excellent customer service. In reward, they are offered enough referrals to ensure that their success grows even further.

Allow me to share an example with you that highlights this connection.

When Lawrence Lo and his business partner, Ken Choi, opened Summit Garden, they had a vision and a plan to make that vision real. Their three step strategy has helped them to pack their restaurant on a daily basis. It includes: a consistently exceptional quality of Cantonese style food; impeccable service; and a friendly, comfortable dining environment. I know that it works, because my wife, Kelly, and I are frequent customers.

The first evening that we ate at Summit Garden, Lawrence made a point of visiting us at our table. He introduced himself and explained his menu. At the end of the best Chinese dinner that either Kelly or I had ever had, he made a point of sending us a complimentary dessert. Then he came back to the table to ask how we felt about the food, service, and presentation. Kelly and I went back a few days later and were, again, very impressed.

Within days we had taken friends to Summit Garden. By now, many of our friends have joined us for meals there. Obviously, many of the restaurant's customers feel the same way. Despite the presence of many other Chinese food restaurants in a relatively small area, Summit Garden is always busy. When satisfied customers talk about Summit Garden with their friends, they are making a referral. Those referrals have made Summit Garden a resounding success.

This success is founded in a basic principle of sales psychology. When you offer your clients extraordinary service, you create a need in them to reciprocate. They need to feel that they are giving you as much as you are giving them. Often, this need will not be satisfied merely by paying for your product or service. The payment is compensation for the service or product they expect. It is not compensation for whatever extraordinary efforts you have made in delivering that product or service. When you treat people exceptionally well, they want to treat you exceptionally well in return. In psychology, this is known as the "***law of reciprocation.***"

Referrals offer clients a way to repay your unusually good service. Most clients are happy to be offered this opportunity to do a service for you. However, you must give them this opportunity by asking them for the referral. If you cannot bring yourself to ask for referrals, it is quite possible that you will build a wonderful relationship with existing clients, and yet find yourself struggling to find new prospects. For the most part, clients will feel happy, but they will not be conscious of their need to do something to make you happy in return. It is your responsibility to bring this need to their awareness by asking them for referrals.

Clients may occasionally volunteer a name to you, but they will not do it often enough to allow you to build your business. Whether you are an entrepreneur, a dentist, a sales representative, or an accountant: if you want referrals, ***you must ask for them***. The ***biggest secret*** for getting more referrals is simply to ask for referrals more often and in more ways.

Chapter One explores the psychology of referrals from the client's point of view. Essentially, it demonstrates that giving referrals helps clients to feel good about the business they have transacted with you. All clients worry about the decisions they have made. Buyer's remorse is the feeling they get when they think they have made a bad decision, or made a good decision too quickly. To help them evaluate their decisions, they seek facts and arguments about the deals they have made. They also check to see if people they respect would have made the same decisions.

This evaluation process is much the same as the process that clients must go through when you ask them for a referral. As part of your request, you will talk about the reasons they have chosen to do business with you and the reasons their friends might also benefit from your product or service. As you talk to your clients about their concerns or hesitations in giving referrals, you will allow your clients to deal with any 'buyer's remorse' before they become aware of it. When they list the reasons they might refer you, or the things they might say in referring you to their friends, your clients will practice selling their friends on your services. They will also convince themselves that they have made a good decision in doing business with you.

Similarly, when they make a referral, they are inviting a friend or colleague to share their judgement of you and the services you provide. The **Law of Social Acceptance** describes the common human need to have our judgements shared and reinforced by others in our community. When a client's referral results in new business for you, it also results in social validation for your client. Someone else shares their opinion of you and your service, reinforcing their own wisdom in doing business with you. The client will feel good, the referred client will feel good (because you will be asking him or her for referrals), and you will feel good. Referrals are, therefore, an excellent way to cement your relationship with current clients while growing new business.

MOVE BEYOND FEAR

Will the fear of rejection or failure stop you from asking for the referrals you need and deserve? Chapter Two looks at the issue of fear, and the costs of letting fear decide whether or not you will ask for a referral. The most intimidating aspect of asking for referrals is dealing with your own internal dialogue. For some people, self-talk ranges from negative to downright debilitating. My "Top Ten" list of reasons not to ask should make you laugh—but it may also make you wince as you recognize some of your own 'top ten' in my list.

You will be even more convinced that it is worth overcoming your fear when you look at the costs associated with avoidance. You could spend a huge proportion of your profit trying to find new business through advertising and marketing. Or you could turn the clients you have into your best, most effective form of marketing and spend your money on something else (a new car, a holiday, new furniture for your living room).

PRACTICE FOR SUCCESS

As I said earlier, asking for referrals makes most people uncomfortable. In the third chapter of this book, we will explore some basic techniques of public speaking. Practicing these techniques will allow you to ask for referrals so persuasively that no one will ever know you were uncomfortable! First, we'll see that breathing correctly is more than half the battle. Then, I will explain how to enhance your natural voice, body language and delivery to get the most out of every request.

In Chapter Four, you will even learn how to make the most of the words you use in every client contact, so that you can ask for referrals without ever asking a direct question. The scripts and language habits in this chapter are subtle reminders to clients that you want and need referrals. Using your enhanced communication skills, you will be able to persuade clients to offer you referrals just by your choice of words. You will even be able to train your assistant or receptionist to put the idea of "referrals" firmly into the mind of every client.

Perhaps the most worrisome part of asking for a referral is the actual choice of words that goes into discussing referrals with your clients directly. What will you do when the client hesitates or objects? How will you know what to say? Chapter Five will present you with scripts for referral presentations. These scripts reflect the real-world experience of professionals from many different fields. They will allow you to practice working your request into the flow of your conversation. With practice, you will sound natural and comfortable with your referrals request.

Through the scripts, you will encounter common objections and rehearse your response to them. You will even face rejection head-on and turn it into success. No single script is right for every professional or every client. To be prepared for many different situations, you must practice many of these scripts. Work with them alone, with a role-play partner, and in front of a video camera. Gradually you will build a repertoire of approaches with which to approach clients.

Of course, your clients will not have practiced their part in the script. But when you have rehearsed scripts from each section, you can be confident that you will have covered all the most common concerns or objections. Using the skills discussed in Chapter Two, you will sharpen your delivery of these scripts to the point where you are virtually irresistible.

GOING FOR IT: GETTING MORE REFERRALS

The scripts in Chapter Five will provide you with a steady stream of referrals. From time to time, however, you may want (or need) a huge infusion of referrals very quickly. Chapter Six will help you to ask for multiple referrals from one client, or to ask many clients for new referrals at once. First, you will practice scripts that ask one client to provide many referrals. While they may seem extreme to some readers, I know that they can work under the right conditions. One young financial planner took my seminar on getting referrals and went on to get more than 100 names from a single client!

I encourage everyone to practice these scripts, even if they seem like overkill. After all, once you have had the experience (through practice) of asking for a dozen referrals, asking for just one or two will be easy! And the more you practice, the more likely it is that you will be able to ask for many referrals when the time is right.

As your client base grows, you may want to generate a large number of referrals by holding a special event. Inviting your clients to attend a Client Appreciation Night is one way to gain many new clients in a single day or evening. A Referrals Contest works on the same principles. You offer a reward (a prize or a special event) to clients in exchange for referrals. More than this, however, you guarantee your clients a chance at something special, because you appreciate their business. And you allow that appreciation to create the kind of atmosphere that lends itself beautifully to referrals.

CONDITIONING FOR CONTINUED SUCCESS

Finally, in Chapter Seven, I will share with you some of the psychological conditioning that helps the most successful people in the world do their jobs better every day. Each day, they increase their motivation, nurture their own confidence, and imagine the success that they will make their own. They are comfortable with themselves and convinced that success is within their grasp. You can use their methods to increase both your productivity and your referrals base.

What are you really afraid of when your stomach tightens at the thought of asking for a referral? Do you feel cornered by the demands of the marketplace? Have you been forced to act in unnatural ways in order to develop a broader client base? Chapter Seven begins with a look at why we sometimes find it difficult to recognize our own sales skills, and to put them to work. As you come to understand why you are experiencing discomfort, you will uncover the hidden limitations that prevent most of us from reaching our full potential for success.

As I prepared the first draft of this book, I was asked to give my four hour seminar on referrals to senior bankers from the Bank of Montreal. I wrote to Doug Dawson, Vice President of Community Banking for London, Ontario, and asked him to describe what separates his high performers from his average performers. Doug's response incorporates everything I believe about the essence of success:

HIGH PERFORMERS TAKE CHARGE AND CREATE RESULTS. THEY MOVE BEYOND THE TRANSACTION REQUEST. THEY LEVERAGE UP OPPORTUNITY AND ASK FOR THE BUSINESS. THEY TURN A SATISFIED CUSTOMER INTO A REFERRAL. THEY MAKE THE TIME TO ACHIEVE SUCCESS.

In other words, the most successful people are the ones who work hard for their customers, and then ask their customers for referrals. Reading this book is your first step towards becoming one of the high performers. You, too, can make the most of every opportunity. You, too, can enjoy a steady stream of new business, all developed through referrals.

Read this book. Think about the ideas you find here. Practice the skills and the scripts. Uncover the hidden limitations that have been standing between you and the success you deserve. Then go out and ask for referrals. Ask as well as you can, as often as you can. Face your own procrastination, your clients' objections and even, from time to time, rejection. In the end, you will be able to ponder your achievements from a beach, a cottage, or a penthouse as you relax and enjoy the benefits of having asked many times for referrals and been rewarded with the natural outcome of all your efforts.

CHAPTER ONE:

WHY CLIENTS LIKE TO MAKE REFERRALS

When I began to compile material for my referrals seminar (and for this book), I talked to many top sales professionals. David Cowper, a long-time sales leader in the insurance field, was one of those professionals.

I asked David if he would be willing to share a winning referral presentation with me and my readers. He was such an accomplished professional that he had no one favourite presentation. David asked for referrals at many different stages in client relationships, and in many different ways. He said he had no set script to share. However, he offered this advice:

ASK YOURSELF: WHAT MAKES ME REFERABLE? THEN BUILD A PRESENTATION ON THOSE QUALITIES.

As you read the pages that follow, keep this one question in mind. It is the key to believing that clients will want to give you referrals. It is the key to making good referral presentations. It is the key to drumming up referrals.

When you identify the qualities that make you referable, you begin to understand why clients want to give you referrals. Why wouldn't they? You deserve referrals. Your clients want to be as fair and reasonable and helpful to you as you have been to them.

Do you believe that giving you referrals will make your clients feel better about themselves and the business they do with you? As soon as you understand that asking for referrals will actually improve your relationship with clients, you will ask for more referrals. As soon as you ask for more referrals, you will have more clients and make more money. Of course, your new clients will refer you to other clients. Asking for referrals is a form of customer service that will lead to exponential growth in your business.

In this chapter, we will look at how giving referrals reinforces your clients' belief that they have made a great decision in doing business with you. Specifically, we will consider:

- ❍ What makes someone "referable?"
- ❍ What motivates a client to give a referral?
- ❍ What scares a client about giving a referral?
- ❍ What can you do to make it easy for your clients to refer you?
- ❍ What follow-up do you need to do with clients who have given you referrals?

By the time you reach the end of this chapter, you will understand clearly how much your clients want to give you referrals. You will know that you can drum up referrals even more often than you close a sale. Go ahead try it out even before you read the rest of the book. You probably have a client who deserves to give you a referral today. Do not be afraid to let your clients help you - and themselves - by referring new clients to you.

ARE YOU REFERABLE?

Getting referrals begins, of course, with providing excellent service and value to your clients. Whatever your field, you must treat your clients with respect and integrity if you wish them to provide you with further business opportunities. There is, quite simply, no way to get a good referral from a client whom you have treated badly.

Think, for example, about my experience with two Mercedes Benz dealerships. The first had benefited from my referrals and gave up the potential for more. The second eventually got both my business and my referrals by working very hard to meet my needs. Let me explain:

Three and a half years ago, I met a Mercedes Benz salesperson named Donna Vande Beek. I walked into the dealership on a Saturday morning, still rather crumpled and sleepy-looking. Despite my appearance, I was treated like a king. Unlike a king, however, I could not ignore a price difference and took my business to a dealership that offered me an unbeatable deal.

In fact, I was so convinced that this dealership would offer 'good deals' that, over the next 3 1/2 years, I referred several friends to them. When I decided to sell my Mercedes and lease a new one, I went to them. The salesman who had worked with me over the past years agreed both to handle the transfer of ownership for my current Mercedes and to arrange for me to lease the service manager's top-of-the-line Mercedes, a car with only 6,000 km on it.

I was very pleased with the deal we negotiated, and arranged to finalize the transfer and pick up the new car on the Thursday before a long weekend. Two days before that Thursday, the salesman called me. Not only had he neglected to mention thousands of dollars in tax that I would have to pay, but he could not deliver the car to me for somewhere from two to four weeks. Naturally, I was upset. I was even more upset when I arrived, as previously arranged, to finalize the transfer of ownership and found that the salesman had not come to work that day.

I was not, however, without alternatives. I walked out of that dealership and telephoned Donna Vande Beek, the Mercedes salesperson who had been so helpful and respectful 3 years before. Donna arranged the transfer of ownership, presented me with several different deals in meticulous detail, and arranged for me to test drive the car I wanted to buy over the long weekend. The deal we settled on was even better than any deal I had been offered at the other dealership.

The moral, of course, is that although Donna's performance did not pay off in the short run (I bought my first Mercedes elsewhere), it will pay off handsomely in the long run. When Donna asks me for a referral, I am happy to suggest that friends, family and colleagues buy their cars from her. Donna's integrity, efficiency and attention shine through every action she takes in serving her clients. In the words of the quality movement, she "exceeds customer expectations" and her reward will be not only her customers' loyalty, but their referrals for new customers.

If, like Donna Vande Beek, you act with efficiency and integrity, you will find that an endless stream of clients are willing to give you a referral. You do not have to be selling Mercedes to give state-of-the-art customer service. Consider the experience of an Avon lady close to me:

For years, I asked my son to take my Avon catalogues to his office. I was sure that I could offer his co-workers great service and great value. They already had one "Avon Lady" in the office, though, and for a long time my catalogues did not make it into my son's workplace.

Then, one Christmas, I got a phone call. Could I put together a presentation for one of the ladies at the office? It was prime shopping season and the regular Avon Lady could not manage a presentation. Everything was set up - except the Avon lady. Needless to say, I packed my bags and set off to give them my best effort.

The evening went very well, and soon my catalogues were bringing in steady business from my son's office. Persistence and good customer service made the difference.

Think about the qualities that you admire in people when you are the client. How many of those qualities do you possess? When you have the answer to that question, you have also answered the question central to this book: "Are you referable?"

To summarize then, referrals grow out of the relationship you have with your client. This relationship must be founded on mutual respect, honesty, and efficiency if it is to become the source of endless referrals. Whenever possible, provide your clients with the kind of outstanding service that will build this kind of strong, referable relationship.

YOUR CLIENTS WANT TO GIVE YOU REFERRALS

If you believe that a referral is a one-way street, where the client gives and you receive, think again. ***When they encounter a professional who is truly referable, clients want and need to make a referral.*** The reasons are two-fold: on the one hand, referring someone reinforces a client's belief that he or she has made a good decision in doing business with you; on the other hand, referring someone allows the client to reciprocate for the extra service you have given him or her. When you ask a satisfied client for a referral, you are helping him or her to feel even better about the business you have just conducted.

As a client, whenever I make a major decision to purchase

a product or service, I risk making a mistake. When I find a product I like and a salesperson I trust, I find it easy to make an initial decision. As you know, decisions - even significant decisions - are likely to be triggered by emotion. No decision is really final, however, until it has been supported by logic. I need to think through all the reasons my decision is the right one. As part of that process, I will probably also want to discuss my decision with people who are close to me. When they affirm that what I have done is right, I can put aside any 'buyer's remorse' and be confident that I have made a good decision.

Now, suppose that the professional with whom I was doing business (a doctor, real estate agent or salesperson) concluded our business by asking if I knew anyone who could benefit from his or her service. I would mentally sort through my friends and family to find a fit. If I did, the professional might ask why I had found a fit. In exploring the reasons I might recommend his or her service, I will have an opportunity to work through the logic of my own decision. I will, in fact, have a chance to overcome any 'buyer's remorse' before I am even aware of it.

When we take this scenario to the next logical step, the professional will follow up on the referral I have made. And if my friend or family member also decides to conduct business with him or her, I will gain in two ways. First, the referred client will reinforce my own belief that I have made an accurate judgment. Second, I will feel good about having shared the benefits of this judgment with someone with a similar need. In this way, my referral is not so much a reward which I offer for good service as it is a mutual benefit.

At the same time, a referral is a way to acknowledge and reward a professional who exceeds my expectations. When a professional does more for me than I could reasonably expect, he or she creates an imbalance in our relationship. Whether consciously or subconsciously, as a client I am left feeling, "This person has done so much more for me than what I paid for: how do I reciprocate?" If the professional in question asks for a referral at this point, he or she gives me a way to say thank you for the service and balance the relationship again.

WHAT WORRIES THE CLIENT ABOUT GIVING A REFERRAL?

Generally, clients whom we have provided with good service would like to refer us to colleagues, friends, and family. As we have seen, giving us a referral will help them to be sure that they have made a good decision in dealing with us. Further, it will help them feel that they have contributed to our well being to the same degree that we have contributed to theirs. Nonetheless, even though they want to give referrals, our clients may not feel comfortable agreeing to a referral request immediately.

Particularly if your request comes early in your relationship, your client may be concerned that he or she simply does not know enough about you to make a referral. Probably they are convinced that they will benefit from your services, but they have not yet had a chance to experience that benefit. They may fear that they are 'wishful thinking' rather than making an objectively good decision. This is a normal consequence of an enthusiastic purchase: when the initial glow wears thin, we wonder if we have done the right thing. The client may want to wait until he or she has gone through a cooling off period and can be objective. He or she may want to be sure that the service you have offered is really as good as it seems.

You may have encountered one of the people who simply never give referrals. While they are not numerous, there are people who will not give a referral no matter how referable you are. You may sometimes win referrals from these clients by using a reverse psychology approach. If you say something like "You're probably one of those people who do not believe in giving referrals. My most critical client was like that once. Now he's my best source of referrals. Don't give it another thought."

Conversely, the client may want to give you a referral, but be worried that he or she will say the wrong thing. A sale has been described as a transference of enthusiasm. Sharing our own enthusiasm inevitably involves some risk. When others do not share our emotion we may feel foolish or rejected. Happy, satisfied customers may not want to risk their good feelings. They may fear being misunderstood or contradicted.

When you ask a client for a referral, you are, no doubt, all too aware of your own fears of rejection. It is helpful to remember that giving a referral also exposes the client to a certain amount of risk. He or she may feel the need to speak directly to the people referred. Maybe he or she is afraid of not knowing what to say or how to say it. And even satisfied clients may feel that they cannot trust you to do a good job for others yet (we have all had relationships that started out great and went downhill). Remember that clients have reasonable concerns, and pick the time and the way you ask for referrals with sensitivity. Just make sure that you do ask for referrals.

PREPARING YOUR CLIENT FOR SUCCESS

If you understand that your client is likely to be nervous about giving you referrals, and you respect that discomfort, you will probably be able to help your client overcome it. Imagine yourself in both roles in the following scenario:

> After a sale is successfully completed, the sales representative asks her client if she knows anyone who might benefit from her product. The client shifts nervously in her chair and mumbles, "Um, I don't know. . . Maybe." The sales representative smiles encouragingly but says nothing. "Yeah, I guess so."
>
> "Would you think about that person for a minute?" the salesperson asks. The client nods, relieved that she has not been asked for a name-yet. The sales rep goes on, "What is it about my product that you think would benefit this person?" The client thinks of the benefits she herself expects to receive. Slowly, she lists some of them.
>
> The salesperson goes on. "If you were going to talk to your friend about my product, what do you think you would say?" The client gives her a slightly alarmed look, and then looks away.
>
> "I don't know," she says.

"**But if you did know**, what would you say?" the salesperson prompts. She smiles and adopts the most open and comforting body language she can. The client watches. A moment of silence passes between them.

"Well," the client begins, "I guess I would tell her. . ."

As you can see, this sales representative is very aware both that her client wants to refer her, and that her client is uncomfortable about doing so. She uses a technique common in psychotherapy to help her client overcome reluctance and imagine giving a referral.

Her questions, body language, and pauses encourage the client to reaffirm the value of the service she has performed and consider logically why this service would be of value to someone she knows. ***As the client begins to voice her ideas, she is also shaping a referral presentation that she can use when speaking to the person she has in mind.***

The sales representative will be able to help form this presentation through positive and sensitive feedback. For instance, she will prompt or echo comments that will be helpful. No matter what the client says, the sales representative will be supportive, using sentences like "Yes, I think so, too. You might also want to say. . ." or "In addition to that point - which is very important - you might want to say. . ." ***Within a few moments, the client will not only have developed a customized referral script, but she will have rehearsed it!***

The process begins when you become aware of the reasons for the discomfort your clients show when asked for referrals. With such awareness to guide you, you will be able to help clients formulate referral presentations which make them feel better. Such presentations are also likely to be well-received by their friends or family. When newly-referred clients meet with you, your client will receive validation for his or her referral. When the referred client closes a deal with you, the original client will be confirmed in the wisdom of both her original decision to buy from you, and the decision to give you a referral.

CHAPTER TWO:

PUT FEAR BEHIND YOU

If you work with clients every day, then you will probably see a client today who would be happy to give you a referral. That client is just waiting to be asked. The only thing standing between you and that referral is your reluctance to ask for it. Although you may find thousands of reasons for not asking for referrals, most of them boil down to one hard truth. Asking for referrals is frightening.

Until you recognize that fear is adding bricks to the wall that stands between you and referrals, you will not be able to tear down that wall and embrace your own success. In this chapter, we will look, brick by brick, at the rationalizations, procrastination, and biases that fear uses to stop us from asking for referrals. As you begin to understand your fear, and to see the many ways that it is shared by others, you will begin to overcome it.

Read this chapter if you know that you are afraid to ask for referrals. Read it even if you think that you are not afraid. Fear is tricky. It often masquerades as reasonable concerns or reasons to procrastinate. Don't let it trick you into putting off asking for the referrals that will grow your business.

ARE YOU AFRAID TO ASK FOR REFERRALS?

What happens to you when a successful sale draws to a close? You know what should happen: you have carefully chosen and rehearsed your referral script. But if you are like most people, you dread the moment when you should turn to your client and put your script into practice. You may dread it so much that you never make the request at all.

F.E.A.R.

Zig Ziglar, the famous motivational speaker, calls fear

"False Evidence Appearing Real"

or **"False Evidence Against Reality."**

Your fear is real to you: your hands get clammy, your heart-rate quickens, and your muscles tense. You feel much the same as you would if you were in real, physical danger. I could tell you that there is nothing to be afraid of but in the grip of fear, such assurances are rather cold comfort. Your shaking knees and dry mouth are persuasive evidence that you do have something to fear. You can eliminate that evidence - and the fear it makes you feel - when you change your perception of what asking for a referral involves.

What kind of risk do you take when you ask for a referral? In my seminars on getting referrals, I show participants a slide that suggests that the first time they ask for a referral they have a 100% chance of being:

1 rejected;

2 kicked in the groin;

3 sprayed with mace; and

4 punched in the nose.

Of course, the next slide reassures them that by the third time they ask for a referral, they will have reduced the odds of serious bodily harm by at least 60% and the chance of getting a positive response will rise to 60%. By the fifth time, the odds of bodily harm drop to almost nothing, and the chance of getting a positive response jumps to nearly 100%.

Most people quit before their fifth try.

It is unlikely that asking for a referral will ever cause you bodily harm. Despite the physical manifestations of your anxiety, you probably realize that you are not responding to a physical threat. So why is your heart pounding and your head starting to ache? The worst thing that your client can do, after all, is to say "no," and you've probably heard that before.

If you let your fears make you feel uncomfortable about asking for referrals, your clients may sense that you are uneasy. They, in turn, will start to feel uneasy, and if they feel uneasy, they will reject your request. In other words, you fear that you will be rejected; your client senses your fear and rejects you. This rejection leads to more fear about asking for referrals and, ultimately, to further rejection.

If, on the other hand, you could make yourself feel comfortable about asking your client for a referral, your chances of success would be very high. As I explain throughout this book, the formula for getting more referrals is simple:

1 provide the best possible service and value to your client;

2 be confident that you deserve a referral;

3 know when and how to ask;

4 and be prepared to deal with any hesitation or objection your client may have.

Does it sound impossible? I know it's not because I have already helped thousands of seminar participants overcome their fears and drum up referrals.

Those success stories began with participants who recognized and swept away attitudes that stood between them and the belief that they deserved success. Your success story will begin when you sweep away your own negatives and become confident that you, too, deserve success.

You must begin by discovering which beliefs and fears are standing between you and success. When, for instance, you focus on the reasons a client might not give you a referral, you allow the client to see them too. On the other hand, when you sweep that focus from your mind, you take the first step along the road to endless referrals.

DAN'S TOP TEN "REASONS I DID NOT ASK FOR A REFERRAL"

I am often asked to accompany junior representatives on their appointments. My role is to observe their sales techniques and provide any information they need. As a result of these outings, I have compiled this "top ten" list given by Rookie, who represents anyone not yet comfortable with the sales process. (We will assume this Rookie is male, but female rookies give all the same reasons!)

Reason #10: It Was the Wrong Time to Ask.

Rookie uses this one often, sometimes varying it with: First, I need to prove myself; Maybe I had not earned the right; Maybe they need to see some results. What Rookie really means is: "It was the wrong time for me to ask. I was scared."

Reason #9: I Forgot to Ask

Sometimes Rookie is so happy to make the sale and get the cheque, he just wants to get out the door before the clients change their minds. In the rush to the door, Rookie forgets to give his referral presentation.

Reason #8: I Had to Leave for My Next Appointment

Rookie enjoyed chatting with this client so much, he could not deliver his referral script and still make it to his next appointment on time.

Reason #7: I Had a Brain Cramp

Poor Rookie worked so hard at this appointment that his brain seized up. No referrals here.

Reason #6: I Had a Weak Bladder

Rookie and I once got to the end of a fabulous appointment. The client was dropping names all over the place. . . you have to talk to my parents, I should get this friend or that friend to speak with you . . . I thought that Rookie was playing it smart. He would wait till the end of the appointment and then ask for a list of all the names.

At the end of the appointment, Rookie took the client's cheque. A strange look came over his face. He thanked the client quickly and headed for the door. We had barely gotten into the car, when Rookie stopped at a Tim Horton's doughnut shop around the corner, and rushed in.

A few minutes later, Rookie returned. The strange look was gone. "I'm sorry, but I had to go pee so badly. I was too embarrassed to use the client's washroom."

Come on, Rookie. A person entrusts you with her life savings, but you were embarrassed to ask to use her washroom?

Reason #5: My Beeper Went Off

Rookie was just about to ask for a referral when his beeper went off! He looked down at his pager, the client started to talk about his pager, and before Rookie knew it, he was saying good-bye. Without a referral.

Reason #4: It Was Snowing Really Hard

Rookie has a nice, safe car but he does not like to drive in the snow. He once ended an appointment without a cheque or a referral because he was afraid to either ask or to linger any longer with the client. "Could I come back next week?" he asked. "My wife worries when I drive in such heavy snow."

Reason #3: The Client Fell Asleep

I was sitting in my fourth appointment in the day, trying to appear alert and interested without actually joining the conversation. Rookie was talking and talking and talking. Suddenly, the client's eyelids got heavier and heavier and the client fell asleep at the kitchen table!

We woke the client gently, and suggested setting up another appointment. Rookie did not get a cheque or a referral. And the client did not keep the next appointment. I think it was fear of being kept up at night.

Reason #2: My client passed away.

Wow! Rookie really talked too long that day.

Reason #1: I did not want to offend my client.

Yes, the most common reason offered for not asking for referrals is "I did not want to offend my client." And, it seems that the more letters Rookie has to put after his name (C.A., M.B.A., Ph.D., etc.), the more likely he is to give this excuse.

If you have given your client good service - if you have identified and filled a real need - it is unlikely that you could offend any client with a well-chosen referral script.

IF YOU STILL THINK YOU MIGHT OFFEND A CLIENT BY ASKING FOR A REFERRAL, RETURN TO CHAPTER ONE.

THE PRICE OF NOT ASKING: ALTERNATIVES TO REFERRALS

Reading through Rookie's reasons NOT to ask for referrals, you may have winced once or twice in recognition. Most of us have some fear of asking for referrals and most of us hide this fear behind excuses like Rookie's. It is not hard to find many reasons to avoid asking for referrals. There is only one over-riding reason to conquer our fear and ask our clients for support in building our businesses.

NO MATTER WHAT THE DOLLAR FIGURES INVOLVED, PAYING FOR NEW BUSINESS IS ALWAYS MORE EXPENSIVE THAN ASKING FOR IT.

When we look at the bottom line, we see that referrals are the most cost-effective way to build a business. No matter what alternative to asking for referrals you turn to in your search for new clients, that alternative will cost much more than asking for a referral.

Asking for a referral costs nothing except preparation and determination. The alternatives to asking for referrals all cost money. Whether you buy newspaper advertisements, put your face on billboards, or send mailers to a target list of potential clients, you will take time and money out of your business. This time and money may be adding up faster than you think.

For instance, someone in my own field of financial planning might consider a variety of ways to attract new business. This chart summarizes a reasonable strategy:

APPROACH	COST
Mailer to target list, sent 4 times per year	$300 x 4 = $1,200
Cold-Calling, one hour per month	$100 x 12 = $1,200
Welcome Wagon leads	600 x $2 = $1,200
Billboard space for one week	$1,200
Total in wages and expenditures	$4,800

In this approach, the financial planner takes $3,600 out of his or her wallet and gives up another $1,200 worth of time to pursue new business. Could this pay off in a financial gain? Certainly. Could the same gain have been achieved - spending no money and only a little time - by asking for referrals? Absolutely.

Life insurance professionals tell me that the value of a referral in their business ranges from $1,200 to $6,000 in new business. Business that is, in effect, free for the asking. Let me say that again: referrals represent money that is free to you for the asking.

IF I CAME UP TO YOU ON
THE STREET AND ASKED FOR $6,000,
WOULD YOU GIVE IT TO ME?

IF I WERE GIVING AWAY $6,000
TO ANYONE WHO ASKED ME FOR IT,
WOULD YOU ASK?

You may protest that referrals in your business are worth much less than $6,000 because your typical sales are worth much less. If this is true, then how can you possibly afford the huge costs associated with advertising? Again, I repeat: referrals represent money that is free for the asking.

Would fear of asking stop you from cashing a winning lottery ticket? Every appointment with a client could be your winning lottery ticket.

EVERY REFERRAL IS POTENTIALLY
A SOURCE OF MONEY.

THE ONLY WAY TO ASK IS TO ASK

There are many different words you can use when asking for a referral. But the only way to get a referral is to ask for one. You will not get referrals:

- by hoping for them
- by rehearsing your presentations, then forgetting to use them
- by reading and practicing alone.

IF YOU WANT A REFERRAL, YOU HAVE TO ASK FOR IT.

A good friend of mine, Tony Mergel (former Director of Music at Humber College and a very successful recording studio entrepreneur) had a wonderful saying about procrastination: "***Procrastination is the thief of time.***" If, like me, you also believe that **Time is Money**, then you will see that procrastination steals both time and money from you. Even worse, procrastination can weaken your confidence, determination and motivation.

Remember, procrastinating does not allow you to avoid making a decision or taking action. You have to decide to procrastinate. To decide to procrastinate takes exactly the same amount of energy as deciding to take positive action. But the inner conflicts represented by your procrastination will erode your self-confidence just as water erodes soil at the edge of a river. This book helps you conquer procrastination by breaking the process of getting referrals into manageable steps. As you work through each new recognition, rehearsal plan, or script, you will make choices to act instead of procrastinating.

If, however, you still want to start taking action later rather than sooner, try to weigh the benefits of starting right now. For example:

BRIEFLY WRITE DOWN THE STEP YOU WOULD MOST LIKE TO PUT OFF:

WRITE DOWN ANY BENEFITS YOU THINK YOU WILL GET BY PROCRASTINATING.

WRITE DOWN THE BENEFITS YOU WILL GET IF YOU START RIGHT NOW!

PROCRASTINATION IN DISGUISE: AVOIDANCE BEHAVIOURS

From time to time, we have difficulty recognizing our own procrastination. It is not that we intentionally put off something that we know we should do. It seems, instead, that more pressing needs arise and make unexpected demands on our time. We discover priorities which interfere with the actions we need to take to meet our own goals.

One of the most important psychiatrists of the twentieth century, Erich Fromm, talks about how we let our fears sabotage our efforts to meet goals. Fromm's theory is that our fear leads us to thoughts, beliefs and actions that prevent us from reaching our full potential. These pseudo-thoughts, pseudo-beliefs and pseudo-actions keep us busy, but move us away from the outcomes we desire.

> For example, you might decide that you need to do some cold-calling in order to meet your sales goal. Because it is late on a Tuesday afternoon, it seems reasonable to defer the cold calls to another day. You decide to spend Saturday morning from 10:00 to 12:00 making cold calls. Relieved by your plan, you spend the rest of the week getting psyched up for Saturday morning.
>
> You are psyched and ready to go-right until about 9:55 that morning. Then you look out your front window and notice that your car is dirty. If a client wants to meet with you this afternoon, you will have to drive to the appointment in a dirty car. Perhaps the client will notice, and think less of you. You cannot afford to make a bad impression on a client. Just in case a client makes an appointment with you, you had better get the car washed.

Of course, the car wash is busy on Saturday morning. The clock ticks along, eating up the time you had hoped to spend on cold-calling. Even worse, once the outside of the car is clean, you notice how dirty the interior is. What if you need to drive a client somewhere later today? You decide that you must have the interior cleaned before you can leave the car wash. The clock is still ticking.

When you finally return home, it is past noon and you have other things to do. You have now lost the two hours you planned to spend on cold-calling and any sales that would have resulted from those calls.

In this scenario, the pseudo-thought is that you will find a client who will object to your dirty car; the pseudo-belief is that the car must be cleaned immediately; the pseudo-action is taking the car to the car wash and away from your objectives for the day. You probably have your own set of actions and beliefs that keep you busy, especially when you would otherwise be taking difficult steps towards your goals. What do you do to convince yourself that you do not really need to ask for referrals?

We all have our own avoidance behaviours. We would all rather get referrals without asking for them. Identify the ways you avoid asking for referrals. Then put off your avoidance and start asking for referrals instead.

UNDERLYING BIASES: DON'T BE AFRAID OF SELLING

It may be that your procrastination is caused by an underlying bias against your own profession (and I do mean a lying bias that undermines your ability to sell). Sadly, many people have learned through experience that salespeople succeed by manipulating their clients. If you have been hurt by a con artist (disguised as a sales professional), then you may be reluctant to succeed as a sales professional yourself. This fear of becoming successful could be stopping you from building your business by asking for referrals.

At some point, many of us have encountered a salesperson who behaved like the one in the following example.

> Suppose you go to a furniture store to buy a leather sofa. You are immediately engaged in conversation by an eager salesperson. You tell him what you want, and he immediately tells you how expensive a "real leather" sofa is. He says that you don't really want "real leather."
>
> You tell him that you have done the homework, you know the cost, and you are prepared to invest in real leather. But he goes on to "hard sell" you on the "Super Duper Vinyl/Naugahyde Special Sofa" that looks and feels "just like real leather" at half the price. You're impressed. It seems like a deal.
>
> Then, as he's writing up the sale, you run into a friend who is working part-time in the same store. You ask his opinion of the deal you just made. To your horror, he says, "The store manager wants to get rid of that junk. it looks good under this lighting, but when you get it home, you'll wish that you had bought the real thing. . . The store manager is sorry he ever ordered that model, so he's given a commission on it that is 500% higher than on real leather."

This is an example of the negative manipulation that takes place when a salesperson sells something that is not in the best interest of the buyer, or convinces a buyer to purchase something against his or her will. These sales result in some exceptional benefit, whether it is obvious or hidden, to the salesperson.

Con-Artists Are Not Good Salespeople

Con-artists represent the most serious threat to the reputation, self-image and effectiveness of everyone whose work involves selling a product or service.

How do people feel after an encounter with a con-artist? They have spent too much time and too much money buying a product or a service, and will find it difficult to trust even the most scrupulous salesperson in the future. Specifically, it takes twice as much ***time*** to buy something from a con-artist. First, it takes extra time for the con-artist to convince you against your better judgment. Then it takes extra time for you to repurchase the product or service the proper way, from a more ethical salesperson. Usually, it also costs twice as much ***money*** to buy something from a con-artist.

After being victimized in this way, it is likely that you will place a question mark after every statement made to you as part of a sales process. Even when you know that the statement is true, or that the salesperson is honest, you will feel ***distrust.*** A con-artist's victims are likely to have lasting difficulties relating to sales professionals. If you have a client who has been "conned" into a bad purchase, it may take a long time for that client to come to trust you. You will have to show extra sensitivity and responsiveness for a long period before you can replace the image of "con artist" with the image of a helpful sales professional.

If you yourself have suffered from dealing with a "con artist," you may need reassurance that most salespeople are not con artists. Having once suffered from negative manipulation, it may be hard for you to believe that you can - and should - set out to convince someone to buy your product or service. If you have these kinds of doubts, you are unlikely to ask your clients for referrals. Before you can drum up referrals, you need to ensure that you have a positive attitude toward the element of manipulation present in all sales.

PRACTICE POSITIVE MANIPULATION

Manipulation is often treated like a nasty word. But most of us will admit, when pressed, that there have been times when we needed to be talked into something that proved to be extremely good for us. Even this book could be seen as an instance of manipulation. Of course, the big winner in this manipulation will not be the person who sold you this book; it will be you after you start getting an amazing number of referrals.

Think of it this way. Let's suppose that you have injured your back. For a certain period of time, you are in a great deal of pain. You walk around with a distorted posture, your face locked into an almost permanent grimace. Finally, a friend suggests that you make an appointment with a chiropractor. Since you have never been to a chiropractor, you are nervous and skeptical. But at this point, you will try almost anything to free yourself from pain. So you visit the chiropractor. After an examination, she tells you that "Your spine needs to be manipulated into proper alignment." And she is right. As soon as she manipulates your spine, you feel instant relief. Her manipulation does not leave you feeling used; it leaves you feeling better able to cope with the demands of your life.

Successful sales transactions are 100% this kind of positive manipulation. A client who has not yet made up his or her mind is "manipulated" into seeing the benefits of a particular product or service that will be in his or her best interest. When your manipulation leaves your client feeling better than he or she felt before, you can reasonably expect that client to want to give you the first in an endless stream of referrals.

HANDLING REJECTION

Even reasonable expectations are, however, wrong sometimes. Inevitably, you will encounter clients who say "no" when you ask them for referrals. While this will not happen most of the time, it will happen some of the time. Your fear of rejection is founded on the reality that your requests for referrals will sometimes be rejected.
The best way to deal with this fear is to think carefully and clearly about what this kind of rejection means.

Often, after we have presented our product or service as clearly and attractively as possible, we are disappointed when a client chooses not to do business with us. This decision may be based on many factors. "NO" may mean "not at this time" or "not the product I need most" or "not something that I can afford." Often, it means "I don't KNOW enough about you or your product to make a decision." No may actually be an invitation to educate a prospect further, to help him to know enough about you to decide to do business with you.

What we hear, however, is usually more negative. We hear "NO - NOT FROM YOU." We take the decision and turn it into a personal rejection. And then, based on this false perception that we (and not our products) have been rejected, we build a wall of fear between us and our next prospects.

If, on the other hand, we think about why a client might actually say "no" to us, we can see that even a failed sale might lead to successful referrals. If you have clearly outlined the features and benefits of your product from the perspective of the clients' best interest, the clients are probably saying no because: a) they don't believe they need the product; b) they don't need it now, but they might need it in the future (and will make the investment then); or c) they really cannot afford it. If circumstances change in the future, these clients will call you because they are comfortable with the relationship you have established. Sales is about making a relationship work so that, ***at any point when it becomes appropriate***, a sale can and will be made.

Within any good sales relationship, whether or not an actual deal has been made, you will be referable. Good sales relationships are possible because you separate rejection (of a sale or of a referral) from rejection of you as a person. The most important word of all is not rejection, but N-E-X-T. If you are confident that you have chosen a sales style that is good for you, that you have treated your clients with integrity and respect, and that the benefits of your product outweigh its cost, you will win both sales and referrals from some of the NEXT prospects you meet.

CHAPTER THREE:

THE SKILLS YOU NEED TO DRUM UP REFERRALS

Now you are one hundred percent convinced that you want to ask your next customer for a referral. But you want to do it right. How can you ask in a way that gives you the best chance for success? Experts overwhelmingly agree that it is how we present ourselves - not what we say - that is most important.

Our ability to look, move, and sound convincing is far more influential than our words. You must make sure that the way you look, move and sound encourages clients to give you referrals. When you practice the techniques outlined in this chapter, you will look and sound exactly like someone who can drum up referrals.

Yes, the ability to look and sound persuasive can be learned and practiced. It does not have to come as an innate talent. All you must do is work on skills which include:

- developing a well-pitched, persuasive voice
- using body language effectively
- working with videotape to improve your performance
- using language to prompt spontaneous referrals.

It will take work to practice these skills enough to make them a normal part of the way you relate to clients. It would be much harder, however, to ask for a referral badly, or to not ask at all. By developing the skills you need to be convincing you will dramatically improve the chance that you will drum up more referrals than you had dared hope.

FIRST, TAKE A DEEP BREATH

The single most important factor in determining how we look and sound is the quality of our breathing. When we take a deep breath, our backs straighten, our muscles relax, our skin tone improves and our voice flows freely and forcefully. Breathing correctly allows us to look and sound our best.

Try it right now. Stand or sit straight enough so that you can easily push out your diaphragm (it is the large muscle above your stomach). Feel the air flow through your nostrils, down your airways, and into your lungs. Are you filling up like a balloon? If you are breathing deeply, your belt should tighten as the lungs fill and the diaphragm expands. Hold the breath for several seconds (more if you already practice deep breathing exercises). Then exhale, slowly and gently. Allow the air to move up from your diaphragm, flow past your lungs, and quietly leave your mouth. Take a moment to observe your feelings as you begin the next breath. Do you feel more relaxed and focussed already?

You breathe every minute of every day. If you don't breathe well, your voice will be high pitched and tense, your muscles tense, your colour poor. If you practice taking good deep breaths, you will gradually be able to control your breath effectively, even in situations where your focus is on other things. And while you practice good breathing, you will be able to prepare both your body and your mind for the challenges before you.

One good exercise is the 8-8-8 method. It is simple: you inhale for a count of 8, hold your breath for a count of 8, and exhale for a count of 8. You may practice sitting still (and straight), standing still or walking. If you choose to walk, you can count steps instead of seconds. Practice this cycle - inhale, hold, exhale - eight to ten times. If you are having trouble, reduce the count to four or six; if 8 comes easily, try holding your breath for 16 counts instead. When you have finished your practice session, you should feel relaxed, focussed and alert. You will be ready to meet with a client, make a sale, and leave with a list of referrals!

MAKE THE MOST OF YOUR VOICE

You may know someone with a great voice, a voice so smooth and assured that it makes everything he or she says sound absolutely convincing. Just as some folks can eat whatever they want without gaining weight, some people speak well without ever doing a vocal exercise. For most of us, however, exercise is necessary, whether we want a great figure or a great voice. If you want to sound like someone who deserves a referral, think about giving your vocal "muscles" a workout.

The first "muscle" you need to consider controls the pitch and volume of your voice. Your voice will have a natural pitch, which may be either high or low. As you become nervous, the muscles in your throat tense up. It is likely that your voice will also become tense and its pitch will go up. You can combat this by doing the deep breathing exercises described above. This will relax your voice and deepen its pitch slightly.

When you are sure that your voice sounds relaxed, you will also want to use your new breath control to raise or lower the volume of your voice at key points in your presentation. Raising your pitch and volume slightly will give the point you are making a sense of excitement; lowering your pitch and volume will lend it an air of seriousness and authority. Such variety will also help your client stay focused and attentive.

Other vocal muscles can also be worked to increase the effectiveness of your delivery. Good timing is always important: in speaking, good timing means manipulating the pace of what you say and when you pause. ***A moment of silence can and will attract as much attention as a shout*** (and is generally much more professional). Try pausing before you deliver an especially important point. I can guarantee that your client will look up at you, waiting for whatever comes next.

Rushing, on the other hand, almost always sounds suspicious. People rush when they are nervous (lacking confidence in themselves, their product or their sales pitch). If you are nervous (before asking for a referral, for instance), focus on slowing your breathing and the pace at which you speak. While it may sound unnatural to your own ears, if you practice it will sound assertive and relaxed to your client.

Inflection and accents vary the emphasis and speed of your voice within a sentence. They are important in adding interest and meaning to what you say. For instance, if asked about your competition, you might reply that "They are not bad." However, the tone of your voice and the way you drag out the word "bad" allow your client to hear more than you have said. He or she will understand not only that the competition is bad, but that you are too professional to come right out and say so.

Generally, tone and inflection allow us to reinforce, change, or undercut the meaning of the words we choose.

Accents work much the same way. When we accent a particular word, we emphasize its role in a sentence. To understand how accents can change meaning, try the following exercise. Say this sentence out loud six times, changing the word you accent each time:

I DIDN’T SAY IT’S A BAD IDEA.

I DIDN’T SAY IT’S A BAD IDEA.

I DIDN’T SAY IT’S A BAD IDEA.

I DIDN’T SAY IT’S A BAD IDEA.

I DIDN’T SAY IT’S A BAD IDEA.

I DIDN’T SAY IT’S A BAD IDEA.

As you will have heard, changing which word is emphasized or accented also makes important changes to the meaning of the sentence. When you practice a sales or referral presentation, be sure that you are aware not only of what the script says, but of what meanings your voice is adding or changing as you speak.

BODY LANGUAGE

In every face-to-face conversation, two sets of signals are exchanged. The obvious exchange takes place through words; the less obvious signals are exchanged through body language. Body language consists of the signals we send one another through:

- eye contact
- movement, and
- body positions

During congruent presentations, your body is saying "Give me a referral" as clearly and openly as your words. And your client's body language is asking for the opportunity to give you referrals. The discussion that follows will help you ensure that your own body language is congruent with your message, and that you are able to read the signals that clients are sending you.

First, though, you need to be aware that body language differs greatly from one culture to another. If you are having trouble communicating with a client, consider whether cultural differences are likely to be creating barriers for you. Although you both may be speaking fluent English, your body languages may be completely different.

You must also remember that reading body language is not an exact science. Your reading of particular signals depends on your knowledge of the client, the situation, and the total effect of all the signals you are receiving. For example, you might ask for a referral. The client says, "Yes, I'll definitely give you a few names. Just let me think about it." However, the client's body language might tell a different story. If he has crossed arms, crossed legs, shows you the bottom of his shoe, or shakes his head "no" and looks away, you can bet that you are never going to get those referrals.

Remember: People make minute changes from moment to moment. Those changes have meaning if you have the skills to interpret them.

READING THE BODY'S LANGUAGE

The following is a list of possible meanings for a variety of common gestures. As we have already said, the exact interpretation of a client's body language depends on your ability to recognize signals and combine their meanings appropriately.

Positive Body Language: In general, these signals are easy to recognize. They could include: a smile; a wink; a "yes" nodding of the head; the client reaching for a chequebook, etc.

Crossed Arms: This signal is the subject of much debate. My own guidelines are that crossed arms could mean: cold hands; sore back; negative feelings; detachment; or fear. It would be difficult to interpret crossed arms as a positive sign.

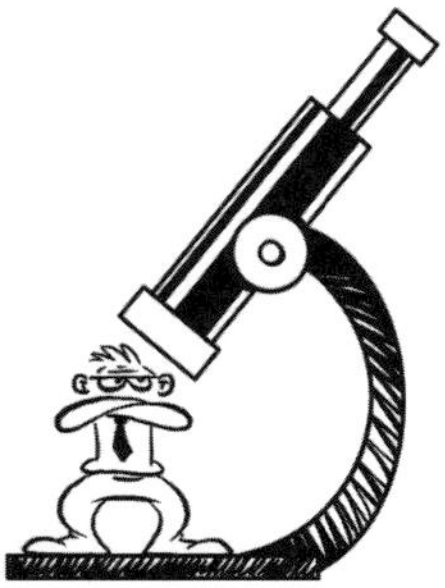

Crossed Legs: Sometimes, crossed legs are a sign of comfort. Watch out, though, if the crossed legs end with an arched foot showing "the bottom of the shoe." This could be a very defensive posture.

Covering the Mouth: "Speak no evil." Most of us are subject to a conscience that tries to stop us from telling lies. On one level, it will do this by causing a hand to rise to the mouth. Regular liars may overcome this mechanism, as will pathological liars - the few people who have no sense that it is wrong to tell lies.

Clenched Fist, Muscle Tension in Jaw, Wrinkled Brow, Client Runs Away: As you have probably guessed, these signals indicate strongly that your client is uncomfortable. You are causing stress, and until you can provide more comfort, you must stop the selling process.

RESPONDING TO YOUR CLIENT'S NEGATIVE BODY LANGUAGE

When your reading of body language tells you that your client is becoming unreasonably stressed, you must stop selling.

One of the best ways to relieve the stress is simply to ***change the subject.*** Three ways to change the subject are:

1 Drop your pen. Pick it up. Make a comment that is not related to your product. For example: You drop your pen. As you bend over to pick it up, say, "The last time I bent over to pick up a pen, I ripped my pants from stem to stern. I'm pleased to report that I didn't rip my pants." When laughter subsides, return to selling.

2 Look at your watch and change the subject. For example: Look at your watch. Say to the client, "By the way, I almost forgot to tell you. . ." Insert a completely unrelated story. If you have trouble

improvising at moments like this, prepare two or three stories in advance and tell the one that is most appropriate.

3 Say "Something just occurred to me." Use this phrase to introduce something related or unrelated to the product you are selling. This gives the client some "mental breathing room."

WHAT DOES YOUR BODY LANGUAGE MEAN?

WHAT DOES YOUR CLIENT'S BODY LANGUAGE MEAN?

MAKE BODY LANGUAGE WORK FOR YOU.

VIDEOTAPE: EVALUATING YOUR VOICE, POSTURE AND BODY LANGUAGE

Whenever you make a presentation or respond to a client, the client "reads" your body language while you are speaking. You, however, may be unaware of some of the things you are saying with your body. How can you focus on your words and your body language at the same time?

You can try to adopt what psychologists call a "meta-position." In essence, you can try to be in two places at once, to be both yourself and a "fly on the wall" able to watch yourself and your client interacting. As you may imagine, the "meta-position" requires a great deal of discipline and mental dexterity. It is not easy to focus simultaneously on what you are saying, how you are saying it, and how your client is responding.

A more straightforward approach to evaluating your own body language is to videotape yourself as you role-play a presentation. If you are like most people, you will resist this suggestion. You may agree in theory that videotape provides valuable feedback that is not available any other way. You may even agree that videotape could allow you to make quantum leaps forward in improving your voice and delivery. But. . .

MOST PEOPLE ARE AFRAID OF VIDEOTAPE.

I'm sure you can already imagine it. You set up the camera. You role-play your presentation with a partner. The videotape picks up every "um...and, uh...and uh" that you say. It also picks up every slouch, twitch, and incongruence in your posture and body language.
In short, it shows you everything you do not want to know about how you might look to a client. Videotape forces you to sit in the client's chair and evaluate what you see.

Watching yourself on videotape can also be the most dramatic way to bring about massive improvement in your referral presentation in a relatively short time.

The best salespeople constantly work to improve their presentations. Like them, you should look to videotape to provide "the truth" about what you are doing and how well you are doing it. In order to make use of this "truth," you must first make a videotape of yourself asking a role-play partner for a referral. It is very important that you follow each of the steps in the following action plan, in the order they are listed. Do not stop between steps. Do not stop if you make a mistake. Plow through your referral script as if you were sitting face to face, knee to knee, belly to belly and wallet to wallet with a valued client.

USING VIDEOTAPE FEEDBACK

1. Find a like-minded individual who will invest one day per month to role-play your sales presentations with a video camera.
2. Set aside a day to videotape. Commit to that day.
3. Arrange to meet at a mutually convenient location.
4. Beg, borrow, rent or buy a video camera and lots of blank tape.
5. Outline the specific outcome that each person desires.
6. Bring a copy of this book.
7. Practice the referral scripts in the next chapters. Focus on the scripts that best suit your personal selling style.
8. Design your own "ultimate" referral presentation and practice it!
9. Get together at the appointed time and place. Role-play your presentation a minimum of 5 times, or until you are completely satisfied with your delivery.
10. Take a short break.
11. Turn on the videotape and tape your presentation.
12. When you are finished, move on to the task of role-playing and recording your partner's sales presentation. Do not review your own performance.[1]

[1]The reasons for not reviewing your performance are twofold. First, you need time to mentally distance yourself from your performance. This will help you to form an objective opinion. Second, you need to relax so that you may evaluate the videotape logically.

WATCHING YOUR VIDEOTAPE

Videotape will show you your posture, mannerisms, and body language as they appear to your clients. It will also let you focus on the sound of your own voice as you go through a referral presentation. In order to evaluate all these aspects, you will have to watch the videotape many times, focusing on a different aspect each time.

After you have watched the videotape through once to gain an overall impression, press the rewind button. The second time you watch, focus on your posture and eye contact. Consider the following questions:

- ❍ Are you sitting up straight, looking confident, relaxed and ready to make a sale?
- ❍ Are you making appropriate eye contact with your role-play partner? Staring intently can make your clients nervous; avoiding their eyes will make you seem nervous.
- ❍ Are you blinking constantly? A few blinks are normal, but too much blinking may suggest that you are under stress or being less than honest.

When you have thoroughly evaluated your posture and rapport with your client, press the rewind button again.

This time, look at all the aspects of body language described in this chapter. How positive is your own body language? Does it reveal the discomfort you no doubt felt at being videotaped? Check for the crossed arms and raised sole that often signal stress or discomfort. Remember, while your client may not be conscious of your body language, he or she will respond to it on a subconscious level.

A referral is, in some ways, a personal endorsement that brings with it some personal risk. Your success in getting more referrals depends on assuring your client that you are comfortable and confident.

More specifically, your movements and body language may also reinforce some points and minimize others. As you watch the videotape yet again (by now the presentation you chose to practice will be indelibly etched in your memory), evaluate the effectiveness of any gestures you may have used. Are they overbearing or are they too small to be noticed? Make sure that any forceful or attention-getting movement is appropriate to its context in your presentation.

Finally, you must "watch" the videotape with your eyes shut. This will allow you to focus all your attention on the sound of your voice. As you listen to the tape (probably several times), think not only about the way you sounded, but about alternative ways of presenting each statement. You may wish to use a cassette recorder to immediately record these alternatives and compare them to your performance in the videotape.

When you put the videotape away, treat yourself to a reward. Analyzing your own body language and voice is difficult, and sometimes nerve-wracking. On the other hand, knowing that you have thoroughly evaluated and practiced your delivery allows you to focus completely on your client and his or her needs and reactions. And that focus is likely to win you more referrals than you might have thought possible.

CHAPTER FOUR:

THE EASIEST WAY TO ASK FOR A REFERRAL

You now know how to shape your delivery of a referral presentation to give you the best possible chance of success. You have a new awareness of the significance of breathing, vocal techniques and body language. You are ready to move on to the finer points of knowing when and how to ask for referrals.

The easiest way to ask for a referral is simply to use the various forms of the word "refer" as often as possible in every conversation you have with a client or prospect. Using the word "refer," "referred," or "referral" in conversation alerts clients to the fact that other clients have been eager to share your expertise and service with their friends and colleagues.

Even your receptionist or assistant can use forms of the word "refer" to predispose your prospects and clients to offer to refer you to their friends and acquaintances. This strategy is exceptionally flexible, effective and easy to use. Try it as soon as possible. You'll find that you begin to drum up referrals even before you finish reading and rehearsing the more formal referral scripts.

LANGUAGE HABITS THAT WIN REFERRALS

You can develop the one habit that will drum up referrals without your ever asking for them directly. All you have to do is to use the word "referral" more often during your conversations with clients. Yes, I really mean that: just using the word "referral" makes it more likely that clients will volunteer to refer friends and relatives to you. Let me repeat:

WHENEVER YOU HAVE THE CHANCE TO USE THE WORD "REFERRAL" IN A SENTENCE—USE IT!

USE THE WORD "REFERRAL" IN A SENTENCE WHENEVER YOU CAN.

NEVER MISS AN OPPORTUNITY TO USE THE WORD "REFERRAL" IN A SENTENCE.

If you are not yet at a stage in your relationship with a client when it would be appropriate to directly ask for a referral, simply slip the word "referral" into your conversation. A client with sophisticated listening skills will pick up the implied suggestion quickly. A client with less-sophisticated listening skills may need to hear the word "referral" more often before responding with a referral. With practice, you will find the most appropriate ways and frequency to use the word "referral" in normal interaction with clients. As with other techniques in this chapter, you must practice.

FOUR STEPS TO BETTER USE OF THE WORD "REFERRAL"

1 Write a statement that uses the word "referral" as you want it to relate to your business and personal communication style. For example, "Most people select a Financial Planner through the referral of a friend."

2 Using a tape recorder, practice the statement by repeating it at least 100 times. When you are working through the best way to deliver the statement, practice at different speeds and volumes; work on placing emphasis on different words.

3 Once you have a "lock" on the ideal presentation, again practice it 100 times. The purpose of such an excessive approach is to make this presentation an intimate part of your autonomic speech function. In other words, you want to practice so much that these words will come naturally to you.

4 With a partner, practice the delivery of the statement with an eye toward refining body language and congruence. Allow your partner to be very picky.

The scripts in the next chapters will give you some good ideas about what to say when asking for a referral. They deserve your attention. They will not, however, get you referrals all on their own. Remember as you read them that they must be delivered in a voice that sounds confident and a body language that says "I deserve a referral." You will earn more referrals - if you practice hard to make your voice, your body and your choice of words reflect the quality of the work you do for your clients.

❍ Work with the sample presentations in the next chapter.

❍ Find the presentation with which you are most comfortable or write one of your own.

- ❍ Practice it until it comes naturally to you.
- ❍ Use it constantly.
- ❍ Strive to improve it.
- ❍ Monitor your results.

WORK THE WORD "REFERRAL" INTO EVERY CLIENT CONTACT

This first set of scripts will demonstrate how easily the word "referral" can become a part of every encounter you have with clients. By using the word "referral" as often as possible, you can suggest that clients offer you more referrals without putting your rapport at risk. Even new contacts or people who don't close a deal with you may end up giving you valuable referrals. For example, let me tell you what I heard the first time I called my chiropractor, Pat Hewitt.

A lady named Karen Legere answered the phone and identified herself as the receptionist. Her first question was, "May I ask who **referred** you?"

"Perry Catena referred me," I answered.

"Well that is great, because we work by referral only."

At this point, I am already very impressed. But Karen went on.

"When Perry Catena referred you, what is it that he said that led you to want to set up an appointment?"

> And again, after I had told her about my back problem, she said, "Well, we have had many people who have been referred to us with the same problem. Dr. Hewitt is very experienced at treating that problem successfully." Then we picked a time for my appointment, and Karen went on, "For your first appointment, we are going to need a bit more time, because you are newly referred."

When I went to my appointment, I immediately noticed a white board in the waiting room. It bore the heading, "People who have been referred to Ridgeway Chiropractic in the last month." Obviously, Dr. Hewitt and his partner, Dr. Mark Fleet, had invested time and energy to ensure that their practice was fine-tuned with respect to seeking referrals, from a client's first contact with the receptionist to the board in the waiting room. Before a client was ever directly asked for a referral, s/he had been given many opportunities to become aware that referrals are important to this business.

Similarly, these scripts will help you to work the word referral into even your earliest contacts with clients and prospective clients.

When a client calls you on the telephone:

Client	Hi, Dr. Smith. How are you?
Dr. Smith	Excellent, thank you. I've had a very busy caseload this week with lots of newly referred patients. How are you?

Client	Hi, Dr. Smith. How are you?
Dr. Smith	Very well, thank you. It's been unbelievably busy here since we told a few patients that we were accepting referrals.

Client	Hi, John. How are things in the world of law?
John	Just great! People have been calling me out of the blue saying they were referred to me and they need my help. It just doesn't get any better. How have you been keeping?

When a client calls you to schedule the first appointment:

Client	Dr. Smith, my name is Gord Athewaste. I'd like to make an appointment with you.
Dr. Smith	That would be fine. May I ask who referred you to me?
Client	My friend, Chester Feeld, referred me to you.
Dr. Smith	Oh, yes, Chester. He was referred to me quite some time ago. When Chester referred you, did he mention my office hours?

When a client calls your receptionist to make an appointment:

(Yes, even your receptionist can solicit referrals without risking rejection!)

Client	Hello. I would like to make an appointment with Dr. Smith please.
Receptionist	Were you referred by a friend or another doctor?
Client	I was referred to Dr. Smith by a friend.
Receptionist	May I ask who referred you to Dr. Smith?
Client	Arnold Piffle referred me to Dr. Smith.
Receptionist	Thank you. Let me get the appointment book.
Client	Hello. I wonder if it would be possible to make an appointment with Dr. Smith?
Receptionist	Yes, of course. Before I book your appointment, may I ask who referred you to Dr. Smith?
Client	I got Dr. Smith's name from the telephone book.
Receptionist	Oh, that's interesting. Most of our new patients are referred to Dr. Smith by existing patients. When would you like to see Dr. Smith?

DURING THE FIRST FEW MINUTES OF AN APPOINTMENT WITH A NEW CLIENT:

Dr. Smith	Before we begin, let me get some basic information. What is the name of the person who referred you to me?
Client	My boss, Andy Kilzmee.
Dr. Smith	Andy has been my patient for quite some time. He was referred to me about five years ago. When Andy referred you, what did he say that made you want to book the appointment with me?
Client	He told me that you are an excellent chiropractor. He also mentioned that you always "crack him up."
Dr. Smith	That's funny. It seems like every new patient that is referred to me says the same thing!
Dentist	When you were referred to me, did your friend tell you that I was a 'painless' dentist?
Patient	Yes, she did. That's why I made the appointment with you.
Dentist	Good. Well, you'll find that **I** feel no pain at all when **I** fix teeth. You, on the other hand, might feel a bit of pain. This is due to the fact that it is rather difficult to be a 'painless patient.'

	All humour aside, and yes that was meant to be funny, if you find yourself experiencing any discomfort, raise your left hand and I will work on another part of your mouth until the discomfort subsides.
	I know this works, because all of the people who are **referred** to me return for follow-up visits and they usually **recommend** a friend or two to our practice. **If it didn't work, do you think we would receive as many newly referred patients as we do?**

At the end of a successful appointment:

Accountant	With all newly **referred** clients, I like to take a few moments to get some feedback. The first question that I always ask is: Are you satisfied with the result of this meeting?
Client	Yes, I am!
Accountant	Great! When you were **referred** to me, the person that **referred** you described the benefits of doing business with me and with this firm. Do you believe that we have lived up to our reputation or is there something else that we could do to fulfill your initial expectation?

RAINING REFERRALS: THE MOST EFFECTIVE WAY TO ASK

You now have the beginning of a toolbox of ways to ask for referrals. The next tool we will place in that box is the single most effective way that I have ever found to ask. In many instances, it will reward you with immediate referrals and it is guaranteed never to result in a "no." I call this strategy the Raining Referrals script. You can use it on the phone or in person, with new prospects and with long-time clients. You can even use it more than once with the same contact (as long as you exercise a little discretion about your timing).

Client	Hello. I'm glad I caught you. How are you?
Super Rep	I'm great. It's been raining referrals. People have been calling me out of the blue to ask for my services.
Client	So business has been really good?
Super Rep	Absolutely. It's been incredible. It's raining referrals. Now, how can I help you today?

As you can see, this script moves to a new level. It implies not only that some clients have made referrals to you, but that most of your clients are eager to send referrals your way. And there is no way to say "no" to it, because you never make a direct request for the referral. You don't even have to use the script yourself; your assistant can say much the same thing when she answers your phone or chats with clients waiting to see you.

Used with good judgement, this script will drum up referrals for you on a regular basis, with very little risk or effort. You might eventually encounter a prospect who says "I know what you're up to. I was at a Dan Bodanis seminar last week and you just used his favourite referrals presentation." Most of the time, however, clients will find themselves mentally searching for someone to refer to you. They'll never know what put it in their minds.

CHAPTER 5:

SCRIPTS FOR ASKING FOR REFERRALS

As effective as it is to integrate the word "referrals" into your regular conversation, there will be times when you want or need to ask a client for referrals directly. A direct request is more complicated and more risky than a subtle suggestion that referrals are a part of the way you do business. When you ask for a referral, you need to combine the best words with the best voice, gestures and body language.

Can you improvise great things to say while trying to read your client and monitor your own voice, gestures and body language? Probably not. You can, however, prepare in advance so that the words which come to you are words which work with your presentation skills to get you referrals.

The scripts in this chapter will help you focus your thoughts and practice the skills you have learned. Read through them all, think about your personal selling style, and pick at least one from each group to practice, practice, practice. When you are confident that you could deliver the presentation in your sleep (but please don't), it is time to find a role-playing partner and turn on the videotape camera.

Don't worry that your real clients won't have read the scripts. Many of their responses will follow the general pattern of the scripts, and you will adapt easily once the scripts have become a part of the way you think. Your practice and preparation will polish your tone of voice and body language until you are virtually irresistible.

If, on the other hand, they say something entirely unexpected, you can answer them directly or move smoothly into a different script. Think how good it will feel to be in control of your appointment, gently leading your client around his or her buyer's remorse and down the path that leads directly to a positive referral relationship.

Can you see yourself asking for referrals with confidence? Can you imagine your clients overcoming their reservations and handing you a business card or a list of names? Using these presentations and your own unique sales style, you can drum up more referrals today and everyday.

DECIDING WHEN TO ASK FOR A REFERRAL

When you are confident that you can deliver them smoothly and sincerely, you will want to try these scripts with your clients. It is important that you introduce them naturally, allowing them to flow into the conversation. This will be hard at first, and you may pick the wrong time to work them in. Don't be discouraged: we all need to learn by practicing and that means that we all make mistakes along the way. Gradually, however, it will become second nature to you to fall into one of the scripts at an opportune moment. And the referrals will come rolling in!

ENFORCING THE LAW OF SOCIAL ACCEPTANCE

We all feel most confident about our judgements when they are shared by those we respect. When a client makes a referral, and that referral in turn becomes a client, both feel better. They know that their judgement of you has been tested by someone else they trust. We call this phenomena the Law of Social Acceptance.

Using selections from the next group of referral presentations, you can help enforce the law of social acceptance. Show your clients how they will respond when their friends and family endorse their good judgement by choosing to do business with you.

The focus of these is on the client's generosity and sound judgment in discovering the benefits of doing business with you. They begin with the client's ability to offer one best friend the chance to benefit from your services. Later presentations offer a vision of the client surrounded by friends and family who are all better off because of referrals he or she has made.

Taking a client into the future to see the results of his or her choices is a technique that psychologists call future pacing. It's useful in combination with many of our other referrals strategies for convincing your client that he or she has made good choices that will be applauded by their family and friends.

IS YOUR playground filled with referrals?

Would you like it to be?

How will you reward yourself when you create this result?

IF YOUR best friend were here right now, would you introduce him/her to the benefits of my products and services?

Best Friend

Super Rep	If your best friend were here right now, would you introduce him/her to the benefits of my products/service?
Client	Sure, I would.
Super Rep	What specific benefits would your best friend achieve by owning my product/service?
Client	It would give them greater peace of mind, and I happen to know they need your product/service.
Super Rep	By the way, what is your best friend's name?
Client	Chester Feeld.
Super Rep	If you were in my position, how would you introduce this product/service to Chester?
Client	I would do this, that, and the other [Client gives you his/her method for persuading the best friend].
Super Rep	You explained that so well, do you think you could say the exact same thing to Chester?
Client	Sure.
Super Rep	If you talk to Chester tomorrow afternoon, do you think it would be okay if I called him tomorrow evening?
Client	Yes!

Allow yourself to have success. You deserve it.

Dan Bodanis

AS A result of your recommendation, whom can I reach down and pull up to the benefits of my product and service?

Lobster Cook-Out

Super Rep	Have you ever been to a lobster cookout?
Client	No, I haven't.
Super Rep	Let me tell you what happens and see if you can picture what I'm describing. First, a very large pot is positioned over an open-spit fire. The pot is then 3/4 of the way filled with water. Once the water is brought to a boil, live lobsters are added. Now, if you have been to a lobster cookout, you would know that they never put a lid on the pot, even after they add the lobsters. The lobsters, with their claws and tentacles, could easily climb out of the pot to safety, but they don't. Do you know why?
Client	No, I don't.
Super Rep	Each time a lobster begins to climb up the side of the pot to safety, one of the other lobsters reaches up and pulls it down. Life can sometimes be like that. As you know, there are two types of people in this world. Those that will reach up and pull you down, and those that will reach down and pull you up. I believe that you are the type of person who would actually enjoy reaching down and pulling someone up. Am I correct?
Client	Yeah, I like to help people whenever I can.
Super Rep	I thought so. As a result of your recommendation, whom can I reach down and pull up to the benefits of my product and service?

What does success look like, sound like, and feel like to you?

Dan Bodanis

I KNOW that today will be the day that you give me his phone number. He obviously needs my help.

I must say that not giving me his number would be a little like telling a child:

"Christmas is coming! Christmas is coming!"

Eventually you have to let that child open some presents.

Now, what did you say his home phone number is?

Christmas is Coming

Super Rep	You have been my Client for a good deal of time, and I believe that we have accomplished a great deal of success. Wouldn't you agree?
Client	Yes, I would definitely agree.
Super Rep	One of the recurring themes in our appointments is your desire to introduce your best friend to my products/services.
Client	What are you getting at?
Super Rep	You have continually mentioned his/her name over the last two years and about eight or nine appointments. You do want him to become my client, don't you?
Client	Of course, I do.
Super Rep	May I ask why you feel that way?
Client	He's always complaining about poor service, lack of punctuality and his current rep's "body odor."
Super Rep	Well, isn't it about time he became my client?
Client	I guess it is.
Super Rep	I know that today will be the day that you give me his phone number. He obviously needs my help. I must say that not giving me his number would be a little like telling a child: "Christmas is coming! Christmas is coming!" Eventually you have to let that child open some presents. Now, what did you say his home phone number is?

How can you help the winds of wisdom to blow favourably in your direction?

Dan Bodanis

IF I were to project myself five years into the future, here's what I would like to be saying to you:

"Thank you so much for helping all of your family, friends, and co-workers to enjoy the benefits of my products and services."

Obviously, my goal is to have each and every one of your family, friends, and co-workers enjoying the benefits of my products and services.

What steps do we need to take to bring this to fruition?

In Five Years

Super Rep	Today, we have set out on a path that will help you to achieve the specific goals that you envision for yourself. How do you feel about that?
Client	I'm glad I finally started.
Super Rep	I'm glad you started, too. Let's dream for a moment. If we were to go out five years into the future, what would you be saying to me about the success that I have helped you to achieve?
Client	I don't know.
Super Rep	If you did know, what would you be saying?
Client	I would probably thank you for providing the guidance and support required in helping me reach my goals.
Super Rep	I appreciate the fact that you are saying that, and I am committed to doing every possible thing I can to help you achieve each and every one of your goals. Would you mind helping me achieve one of my goals?
Client	I would be happy to.
Super Rep	If I were to project myself five years into the future, here's what I would like to be saying to you: "Thank you so much for helping all of your family, friends, and co-workers to enjoy the benefits of my products and services." Obviously, my goal is to have each and every one of your family, friends, and co-workers enjoying the benefits of my products and services.

	What steps to we need to take to bring this to fruition?
Client	I'm not sure.
Super Rep	You have already said that your friends could benefit from my products and services, and you mentioned the fact that in five years you would be thanking me for my help. Are you sure that you would like your friends to benefit to this extent?
Client	Of course.
Super Rep	Okay. We know that not all of your friends will become my clients right away. We should just focus on the people that you feel need me and my products and services immediately. Who is the first person you thought of, right after you made the decision to do business with me today?

If the journey of a thousand miles begins with the first step, what are you waiting for?

Dan Bodanis

LET THE CLIENT DO SOMETHING FOR YOU

Have you offered a client the very best possible service? Did you go beyond the call of duty just to be helpful?

Use these next presentations when you are sure that you have provided your client with the best service you can offer. This group of referral presentations depends on your clients' belief that you have offered them value that exceeds the amount you are charging them. When you have performed some extraordinary service for your client, you deserve to use one of these presentations.

Each of these presentations contains an explicit invitation to the client to do something for you. They encourage the client to obey the "law of reciprocation" by offering you an unusual benefit in return for your unusually good service.

MOST OF my clients refer me to at least two people within three days of doing business.

Instead of receiving surprise calls from your friends I have yet to meet, would you mind if I asked whom you will be referring me to?

It always helps to have some background information.

2 People in 3 Days

Super Rep	Most of my clients refer me to at least two people within three days of doing business. Instead of receiving surprise calls from your friends I have yet to meet, would you mind if I asked whom you will be referring me to? It always helps to have some background information.
Client	Sure. I'm going to tell my brother and my aunt.
Super Rep	In your opinion, what would be important to know about your brother and aunt?
Client	My brother's name is Herman, and my aunt's name is Betsy. They both use your product and I happen to know that they pay too much buying it from their current supplier.
Super Rep	I really appreciate your sharing that information with me. Do you think it would be in their best interest if I were to call and tell them what you just said?
Client	Absolutely.
Super Rep	Great! In addition to Herman and Betsy, who else do you feel would benefit by owning my product, and what time of day should I call them?

MY BEST clients write a brief introduction on the back of one of their business cards.

This introduction is usually a one sentence explanation of the value I can provide.

Business Card

Super Rep	I wonder if you would help me in a very unique way?
Client	Help you in a unique way? What do you mean?
Super Rep	My best clients refer me to their friends in a very special way.
Client	Oh, really, and what way is that?
Super Rep	My best clients write a brief introduction on the back of one of their business cards. This introduction is usually a one sentence explanation of the value I can provide.
Client	What would you like me to write?
Super Rep	You could write something to the effect: This is Frank; he saved my life and he could save yours. [At this point, flash your best smile and pray that your client has a sense of humor.]
Client	So, you would just hand my card to my friend and then what?
Super Rep	On the strength of your recommendation, your best friend would probably be receptive to granting me a small amount of his valuable time to find out if he needs my product or service.

In regard to success, your congruity will speak louder than your words.
Dan Bodanis

BECAUSE I'M
only here for the
next few days,
would you mind
calling to
introduce me?

Call to Introduce Me

Super Rep	John, I will be visiting other people in this area over the next few days. If you were me, whom would you call on?
Client	I think Brutus Buhtkik over at the law office of Dewey, Cheatum & Howe could probably use your services.
Super Rep	Do you know Brutus very well?
Client	Yes, I do.
Super Rep	Would you mind giving me an introduction to Brutus?
Client	I could arrange that.
Super Rep	Because I'm only here for the next few days, would you mind calling to introduce me?
Client	Right now?
Super Rep	Yes. If I can help Brutus as well as you think I can, he will be glad you made the call.
Client	If I make this call, what's in it for me?
Super Rep	Beside the personal satisfaction of helping Brutus, you can ask him that question yourself.

Investing in your own personal development is the best investment you could ever make.
Dan Bodanis

YOUR SUCCESS in sales is determined by many important factors.

Near the top of that list is your ability to handle objections with Poise and Grace.

(Who's Grace?)

OVERCOMING OBJECTIONS: GET THE REFERRALS YOU DESERVE

These four scripts will give you the basic tools you need to overcome a client's initial resistance. The first of these slips the request for a referral into a pleasant anecdote. Similarly, the second script begins by securing the client's agreement with a general principle. Based on that agreement, of course, it moves to ask the client for referrals.

In the final scripts in this section, you will find different ways to overcome lingering skepticism or discomfort. In countering implicit or explicit objections, you will also help your clients to head off any 'buyer's remorse.' They'll leave feeling good about doing business with you. You will walk away with a pocketful of referrals!

THAT ALSO reminds me that I should ask you about the people you will be referring to me.

Who did you have in mind, and why do you feel that they should become my clients?

Silver Dollar Shoes

Super Rep	Thank you for doing business with me today. In my first year with XYZ Co., I had a manager that I really liked and respected.
Client	Oh, really?
Super Rep	Yeah, and that reminds me of a funny thing he used to do with all of the rookie sales people he recruited.
Client	What was that?
Super Rep	He used to make new salespeople walk around with a silver dollar in their shoe.
Client	Why did he do that?
Super Rep	He wanted to make sure that his salespeople were constantly reminded to treat clients with the utmost respect and dignity. He believed that if you did that, those people would go out of their way to be your best form of advertisement. The silver dollar was like a stone in the shoe, a constant little reminder.
Client	I'm not sure I follow.
Super Rep	In the experience of that manager, he found that taking exceptionally good care of his clients led to incredible referrals. His clients would immediately refer him to at least four friends that would absolutely benefit from his product/service. The silver dollar was like the 'stone in the shoe,' a constant reminder to continually exceed client expectation. The referrals that came

	would obviously help that rookie salesperson to 'fill their shoes' with silver dollars.
Client	I understand.
Super Rep	It's funny how you reminded me of I man I have so much respect for, and the way he used to train rookies. That also reminds me that I should ask you about the people you will be referring to me. Who did you have in mind, and why do you feel they should become my client?

Are you exercising your brain for success on a daily basis?
Dan Bodanis

Is Your Net Working?

NETWORKING AND receiving referrals are without question the best ways of prospecting for new business.

Wouldn't you agree?

LEARNING FROM CHILDREN

Super Rep	Networking and receiving referrals are without question the best ways of prospecting for new business, wouldn't you agree?
Client	Yes, I would. What are you getting at?
Super Rep	Driving home from work yesterday, I passed a school yard and I had a major insight.
Client	Really, what was it?
Super Rep	You can learn so much from children. To be successful in life, we must develop an ability to attract and cultivate strong relationships. How does a child develop relationships?
Client	I've never really thought about it. I guess they become friends with one child. That child introduces them to another and so on. Is that what you're getting at?
Super Rep	Exactly. It's so easy for most children to make friends. They just seem to have that 'magic' about them.
Client	Yeah, I know what you mean.
Super Rep	My question to you is: how can we capture, or shall I say, recapture, that magic?
Client	I don't know. Maybe we become 'guarded' as we grow older.

Super Rep	You've got a point there. With reference to exponentially building a strong network of referral business, what steps do we need to take to enable ourselves to 'gather friends' in the same way children do?
Client	That's a good question.
Super Rep	What if we just went through our phone books looking for names of friends that could benefit from the services we each provide?

There are many ways to succeed.
Which way is best for you, and what action will you take?
Dan Bodanis

IF YOU don't know where it is you are going . . .

How can you possibly help others to get to their destination?

IF YOU did know . . .

I Don't Know

Super Rep	What will you be saying to your friends about my service and products?
Client	I don't know.
Super Rep	If you did know, what would you be saying?
Client	You have treated me fairly, and your products are competitively priced.
Super Rep	Thank you for saying that. What effect might your testimonial have on your friends?
Client	I don't know.
Super Rep	If you did know, what effect would your testimonial have?
Client	They (my friends) might want to arrange an appointment and they might end up doing business with you.
Super Rep	Now that wouldn't be so bad. Would it?
Client	I guess not.
Super Rep	How could we accelerate this process?
Client	What do you mean?
Super Rep	Your friends would definitely benefit from the services I provide, right?
Client	Right.
Super Rep	O.K. then, what would be the quickest way for me to contact them to arrange for an appointment?

Client	I don't know.
Super Rep	If you did know, what would be the quickest way for me to contact your friends to arrange for an appointment?

Caring enough to persist will often produce outstanding results.

Dan Bodanis

DON'T JUST do it.

Just do it well!

I GET "boatloads of happily referred people."

Every client I deal with refers me to at least six people.

Those people, just like you, will be skeptical at first.

Skeptics to Boatloads

Super Rep	You sure looked skeptical when we first met. Why did you change your mind and decide to do business with me and my company?
Client	I did business with you because . . . (You have a really big nose, two left feet, a deviated cranial cavity and an ultra-bright smile.)
Super Rep	Great! That's exactly why most people become my client and it is also the primary reason I get 'boatloads of happily referred people.' Every client I deal with refers me to at least six people. Those people, just like you, will be sceptical at first.
Client	Well, I think that it is basic human nature to be skeptical of salespeople.
Super Rep	You're absolutely right! After investing a short amount of time with me, that skepticism evaporates into thin air like (insert your favorite metaphor) fresh baked apple-pie disappearing from the dinner table. The best part is that your friends won't be able to praise you enough for referring me to them.
Client	[Blank stare]
Super Rep	In your opinion, out of the six people you will be referring me to, who would be the first person I need to speak with right now?

If you had to write the ultimate definition of "success," what would you write?

Dan Bodanis

WRITE YOUR OWN PERFECT PRESENTATION

When you have mastered all these scripts, you will have an excellent sense of how to approach clients in many situations. You will have a repertoire of ways to meet objections or take advantage of good feelings to drum up referrals. At this point, you will be able to easily customize your referrals script to reflect your own special strengths and circumstances.

Although you will develop many different approaches as you become successful in drumming up referrals, your most important approach will always begin with an answer to the question: What makes you referable? As top insurance professional, David Cowper, pointed out to me, this is the question that leads most surely to success. When you have absolute confidence that you are referable, your clients will share that confidence.

Think about what makes you referable to your clients. Pick out the most important quality, and write a script in which you use that quality to remind your clients that they want their friends or colleagues to do business with you, too. Variations of this script, combined with the scripts I have provided here, will drum up as many referrals as you can handle.

CHAPTER SIX:

ASKING FOR MORE REFERRALS

Throughout this book, I have encouraged you to drum up referrals as part of every business day. Your single most important source for referrals will be your commitment to asking for them from every client and prospect you meet. From time to time, however, you will want or need to drum up even more referrals. Equipped with your new drumming skills, you may wish to work with groups of clients and prospects. Where do you find groups who might wish to give you many referrals at once? In the pages that follow I will suggest three ways to find or develop groups who will give you referrals.

Your clients already form a group who might offer you referrals. Usually, however, we meet with our clients one on one or in very small groups. It takes a new perspective or a special event to bring clients together in the kind of group that offers opportunities for an outpouring of referrals. You can arrange just such an opportunity when you hold a referrals contest. Inspired by a terrific prize (or prizes) and by your enthusiasm and excellence, clients compete to see who can bring you the most new business.

Friendly competition can take on the character of community entertainment when you gather your clients in one room for a Client Appreciation event. This event not only inspires your clients to offer you new referrals. It reminds them of the unusually good rapport they feel with you and the productive relationship you have developed. It makes clients feel good about doing business with you, and eager to share that good feeling with their friends or colleagues.

Both the referrals contest and the client appreciation event draw on your current client base for new referrals. They attract attention to your desire to grow your business while reinforcing the value you place on your current business relationships.

What if you want to reach people beyond the circle of influence of your current clients? A client base is one kind of community. It exists within a broader community. As you become active and well known in this community, you begin to attract attention. You can offer excellent support to a community group in the same way that you habitually support your clients. The group repays you for your support with an interest in your business. As you nurture this interest, you drum up referrals. These referrals become new links between the community of your clients and the community at large. The more links you encourage, the wider the call of your drum as you seek out new clients.

These three methods of drumming up many new referrals at once all depend on the same principles of reciprocation, social validation, and unusually good service that underlie your efforts to win referrals every day. While you read through the details of how to use these opportunities to maximum advantage, keep in mind these underlying principles. As long as you respect the psychological process that governs a referral, you will be able to adapt details, approaches, and events to suit your personal selling style, type of business, and budget.

THE REFERRALS CONTEST: OFFER YOUR CLIENTS A CHANCE TO WIN

The referrals contest is both an effort to stir up some excitement for your clients and a chance for you to attract well-qualified referrals on a grand scale. The contest rewards the client who refers the largest number of people to you within a specified time. If you choose an exciting prize, many clients will participate because they are happy to help you and they appreciate the chance to win.

How do you hold a referrals contest? Begin by picking a date that is far enough into the future to give you a chance to plan, promote and track referrals. The date must also be soon enough to create a sense of urgency in your clients. With the closing date set, you need to establish the kind of prize that will entice your clients to call you with the names and numbers of their friends and colleagues. In a large city, this prize might be tickets to a major theatre or sporting event, dinner at a fine restaurant, and a limousine for the evening. If your hometown does not regularly feature this kind of entertainment, you might offer a weekend away at a nearby resort. You might even consider picking up the cost of a flight and a hotel to a larger city. The most important factor in choosing a prize is the interests of the people in your client base. Choose something that will inspire the greatest number of clients to their greatest efforts.

WEIGH THE COSTS OF THE CONTEST AGAINST THE VALUE OF REFERRALS

Earlier in this book, we discussed the cost of not asking for referrals and weighed them against the value of each referral. Use the same considerations in deciding how much you can spend on the prize you offer in your referral contest. However expensive the prize might seem at first, it could be the best investment you make. First, the prize will help you to attract a large number of well-qualified prospects, many of whom will soon become your clients. Second, the contest will keep you in front of your clients in a uniquely positive way. Third, the contest may give you a real edge over the competition.

A luxurious, even extravagant, prize says to your clients: "I value you and I value your referrals." Unless your competition is already holding an equally exciting contest, you will have positioned yourself at a distinct advantage. If they come up with a competing contest, even with a better prize, they will only seem to be copying your initiative. Your clients will have already seen how much you value both their business and their referrals. They will know that you put the same creativity and commitment into doing business that you put into designing your referrals contest.

PLANNING AND PROMOTING YOUR CONTEST

The contest begins for you when you establish the need for rapid growth in your business, pick a time frame when you will be able to follow up on a large number of referrals, and set a closing date for your contest. Next you pick a prize or, if you wish, a grand prize and two or three smaller prizes. You will also want to set some basic rules. Will you set a minimum number of referrals (eg. To enter you must refer at least 5 people) to qualify for the contest? What will you consider a referral for the purpose of the contest (a filled-out referral card, a name and phone number given verbally, a prospect who calls and says he or she was referred)? Next, set up a tally sheet, database or other system to track the referrals you receive. Finally, set up a system for thanking each client for the referrals they send you.

Now you must set up a plan to promote your contest. Word of the contest must reach each one of your clients if you are to get maximum value out of it. How you reach your clients will depend on their numbers, geographic locations, and preferred communication styles. You may wish to send a newsletter or announcement through the mail (think of interesting ways to present this using colour, papers or small gimmicks). If you have an assistant to help you or a relatively limited client base, you may wish to phone each client, in addition to or instead of contacting them with a mailer.

Finally, you will want to work news of the contest into all your personal contacts from this point until the contest closing date. Everyone you know should know about the contest. Prepare sample scripts that allow you to work news of the contest into various kinds of contacts with clients and prospects. Practice these scripts as rigorously as you practice your referral scripts. You will now be prepared to offer complete contest details in a range of situations.

Promoting the contest before its closing date is only the beginning. Everyone who participates in the contest will want to know who has won. Arrange to have a photograph taken of your winners accepting their gift certificate, stepping into their limousine, or standing outside the theatre or arena. Ask them to comment on how much they enjoyed their evening out or weekend away. Add a report on the winners to your next newsletter or frame the photograph and hang it in your place of business. After you have held several contests, you may be able to mount a collage of photographs, ticket stubs or programmes. This collage will show everyone who steps into your office how much you value your clients and the referrals they offer you.

CLIENT APPRECIATION: EVENTS TO REMEMBER

You may want to include another kind of event in your collage. Referral contests take place over a period of time and encourage individual clients to come to you with referrals. This is good, because it also gives you a period of time in which you can follow up on all the referrals you get. It is not so good at creating a kind of community spirit within your client base, or reaching every one of your clients with the message that you truly appreciate their business.

If you want to reinforce this sense that your clients are part of a community of shared values (and to drum up referrals) consider hosting a client appreciation event. Such events require more planning and more expenditures than referral contests, but they offer unmatched opportunities to build and deepen your client relationships while cultivating new clients.

Essentially, a client appreciation event is a party that you host. Like other good parties, its success will depend on the right mix of location, ambience, food, entertainment and people. Your first goal is to think about your current clients and plan an event that will be too good for them to miss. Your second goal is to persuade them to bring guests to your event, guests who are not yet your clients. Your final goal is to ensure that the event lives up to your promises and lives on in your clients' memories. If you achieve each of these goals, you can double your client base in a single day!

Imagine this scene. You are in a crowded banquet room at a large hotel near the Toronto airport. Women gather around the guest speaker, eager for an autograph. Many reach out to touch his biceps. The men look on with envy but they, too, are intrigued. The occasion? A "Health and Wealth" seminar I held to express appreciation to my financial planning clients. I spoke on Wealth. My friend, Mohammed Makaway, a four-time Mr. Universe spoke on Health. Several years later, my clients still talk about that evening. When you use your imagination to provide your clients with a uniquely enjoyable evening, they remember for years to come.

PREPARING FOR A MEMORABLE EVENT

As we will we see, successful events like the one described above begin with a vision. No, I don't mean you need to see a psychic. I mean you need to create a clear mental picture of every aspect of the event. Begin with an unshakeable conviction that you have what it takes to offer your clients a remarkable evening and earn a flood of referrals from them. As you develop the details of that evening (or afternoon), incorporate them into an increasingly specific image. Use this image to guide you in crafting an affirmation of your inevitable success.

Your use of imagery and affirmation will set the stage for your success. Staging an event also requires a multitude of decisions and actions. You must find a location, invite speakers or choose entertainment, and select appropriate food and beverages. Most importantly, you must develop and practice an irresistible script for inviting clients to attend your event and to bring guests with them. You must prepare to meet these guests, to get their names and phone numbers, and to persuade as many as possible to meet with you. You also need a system that will allow you to keep track of both referrals and your clients' response to the event.

In short, then, you will need:

1 An absolute expectation of total success!

2 A mental image of the event's positive outcome.

3 A positive affirmation to correspond to that vision.

4 Enough clients and guests to fill the room.

5 An irresistible script.

6 Two weeks of lead-time to prepare.

7 A well-chosen location that shows your attention to detail.

8 Door Prizes

9 A follow-up system for referred prospects.

10 A mechanism for feedback.

IMAGINE AND AFFIRM YOUR SUCCESS

In his best-selling book, *The Seven Habits of Highly Effective People*, Stephen Covey says "Begin with the end in mind." If you can clearly picture a successful client appreciation event, then you can make it happen. Once you create the image of what you want, you can focus on that image. At every step in your preparations, you can draw on that image for inspiration, direction and optimism.

What do you want from your client appreciation event? Five new clients? Fifty new clients? Two hundred new clients? Do you want your current clients to feel more relaxed, enthusiastic or committed to doing business with you? Before you can make this happen, you need to imagine it. Close your eyes, and paint yourself a picture of success. Visit the room you have booked for the event, and look closely at the size, shape, lighting and décor. You'll need these details as you shape a visualisation of that room filled with your smiling clients and their guests. If possible, practice your presentation with the same audio-visual equipment that you will use. Pick out the clothes that you will wear.

It is well known in coaching circles that you need to practice under playing conditions. What is less well known is that you can take enormous strides towards success by practising mentally. Now that you have gathered detailed information about how you can expect your event to look, put that information to work. Create a mental image of the room filled with your clients and their guests. "Walk" from seat to seat around the room, listening to the chatter of your guests as they discuss the excellent service you have provided, or the reasons that prospects should meet with you immediately. Watch yourself as you step to the front of the room and begin to speak.

Can you feel the excitement in your muscles as you begin your presentation or introduce your speakers? You are keyed up, ready to perform at your very best. The adrenaline that courses through your veins is pumping you up, priming you for your best performance ever.

Look around the room, every face turned towards you. This audience is with you; they want to hear what you have to say.

Do you feel energized just reading this? Visualising success is exciting. It is your best chance to put the full power of your imagination to work for you. It works for many of the top athletes in the world. It works for the leading professionals in fields as wide-ranging as surgery, the performing arts, or corporate management. Best of all, this is not the rocky road to success. It is more like flying first class. You can sit in your favourite chair, breathe deeply and close your eyes. Imagine in great detail the best evening of your life. Enjoy it.

AFFIRMATIONS: POSITIVE, PORTABLE REMINDERS

You may now want to spend a large part of each day stretched out in your favourite chair imagining your own success. Instead, you will have to spend much of your day doing other kinds of work and preparing for your client appreciation event. Is there some way you can keep this positive image and the confidence it gives you throughout the day? There is!

An affirmation is a one or two sentence statement that supports or emphasizes the positive outcome that you want and expect. As you will recall from the previous chapter, affirmations work extremely well with positive imagery. In this instance, you will take your positive image of your client appreciation event and use it to create three affirmations. For instance, you might say:

Within the next two weeks, I will book appointments with the seventy-five prospects who attend my event, and I will turn each one of them into a client.

As you look further at your image of success, you will hear a colleague say to you:

You are amazing. I am impressed that you have seventy-five prospects as the result of one client event.

Now, wander through your mental image of the event until you overhear a client talking to the guest he or she has brought to the event:

[Your name] has done so much for me. S/He's really been terrific. I know that when you talk to her/him you're going to be impressed. You'll be glad you chose her/him to work with.

Repeat these affirmations many times a day. Between appointments, driving in your car, putting away the dinner dishes: any quiet moment is a chance to say these affirmations to yourself. The more often you repeat them, the more effective they will be in leading you to actual success at your client appreciation event.

PLANNING THE EVENT

Your most important decision is to choose a location for your event that will prove particularly attractive to your clients and their guests. You may have a location in your community that springs to mind because it will hold some special interest for your clients. Your office or place of business may feature an attractive room for entertaining. If not, you can choose from among the meeting facilities, banquet halls and hotels that would be conveniently located for most of your clients. Pick a location that has the same kind of image you want to project: classy, comfortable and well-prepared.

Book a room at this location that will be filled by the number of people you anticipate will come to your event. It's always hard to judge just how many people will show up. Let's take an example. If 15 clients accept your invitation and you invite them to bring 2 guests each, how big a room will you need? I would book a room that comfortably holds 30 people. My own experience has been that some people inevitably find that something prevents them from coming, often at the last moment. If 10 of the 15 clients who accepted your invitation arrive with 2 guests each, you will have a total of 30 guests. Your room will be filled to capacity.

Have you ever attended a meeting in a room that was far larger than the attendance warranted? A few people cluster near the front, more arrange themselves near the aisles (the better to make a quick escape) and several skeptical souls fill the last few rows of chairs. The speaker tries to make eye contact with the scattered group, but can only see a small proportion at once. Sound bounces around the room, making it feel more empty than it is. This is one situation where bigger is definitely not better.

Avoid this problem. The room you book should provide seating for all your guests, without providing too many empty chairs. When people look around at a full banquet room, they will see a crowd gathered to hear your drumming. They will know that you are in demand. They will feel part of a group sharing the pleasant experience you are providing. Don't be fooled by disparaging remarks about the big fish in the small pond. The big fish has the complete attention of his limited audience. Of course, as your own client base grows, your events will grow proportionately. Soon you will be the big fish in the big pond!

HOW TO INVITE CLIENTS TO YOUR EVENT

Two weeks before your event, you will want to call your clients to invite them to your event. If you call more than two weeks ahead of time, you will have to call again. People forget that they have promised to come, other events in their lives are rescheduled, or new events arise that interfere with yours. If you call less than two weeks ahead, you risk finding that many of your clients already have prior commitments.

Of course, you may have to vary this schedule slightly depending on how many clients you are inviting, how much time you expect them to spend at your event, and how far they will have to travel to join you. If you send out announcements or invitations through the mail, you will have to allow greater lead-time. You'll probably also have to follow up with phone calls in order to get your clients out to your event.

Before you go to the telephone, however, you will want to develop and practice an irresistible script. This script must be so compelling that no client will hear it and want to say, "I'm sorry. I can't make it."

Here is an example of a script that has brought many clients out to my own events:

Super Rep	Hello, Ruth. I'm calling to invite you to a very special event.
Ruth	Oh, really? Tell me more.
Super Rep	I will be hosting a Client Appreciation Night for a select group of people with whom I have had the pleasure of doing business recently. There will be food, wine, coffee, desserts, and special door prizes. The President of our company will be there to personally thank you for placing your business with us. You've got to be there. This will be the A+ of A parties. Can I put you at the top of the guest list?
Ruth	Sounds good, when is it?

Super Rep	I'll get to that in a moment. Before I do, let me tell you about a very special prize that I know you would love to win. You are welcome to bring at least two people who could benefit from our services to this Client Appreciation Night. The person who brings the most people - and remember, you need to bring at least two people to qualify - will win two of the best seats in the house at (name a theatre, sporting event or fine restaurant). The date is Tuesday the 16th, two weeks from today. The location is the Kings Golf and Country Club in the Royalty Suite.
Ruth	I would love to come.
Super Rep	Great! I need to let the catering manager know how much food and drink to order. May I count on you to bring at least two guests?
Ruth	I think so.
Super Rep	I look forward to seeing you on the 16th. Oh, by the way, please call me if you would like to bring more than four people. I will need to let the catering manager know so that we have enough chairs for your guests.

You will want to modify this script to suit the details of your own event. Feel free to design and practice different scripts until you find the one that is most perfectly suited to your selling style.

Make sure, however, that your own script follows the same structure as this one. Most importantly, notice that the date and location of the event are not revealed until your client has had the chance to listen to their favourite radio station: WIIFM.

WHAT'S IN IT FOR ME?

WORKING WITH YOUR VENUE TO ACHIEVE SUCCESS

The location where you hold your client appreciation event speaks volumes about the way you perceive your clients and the way you want them to perceive you. An upscale venue creates the impression that you are successful, thoughtful, and caring. It shows that you have a taste for the finer things in life, and you want your clients to experience those things with you.

As you book your room and plan its set-up, pay special attention to these details:

- Let the banquet manager know that you do not want to host your event beside any event that might detract from it, such as: a wedding, band rehearsal, motivational meeting, stereo clearance sale, or monster truck derby.
- Leave extra space between chairs. Have pens with your name on them placed on each seat, along with your appointment card and feedback sheet.
- If you will need audio-visual equipment, book the best. Hire a professional audio-visual company to

setup your projection screen with a black velvet border. Use an overhead projector with a quick-change spare bulb.

- ❍ Include a water station.
- ❍ If possible, speak from a platform elevated by about 8 to 10 inches. Your Master of Ceremonies can use a podium-based microphone. You should use a wireless lavaliere microphone (lapel microphone). Make sure that it is powered by fresh batteries, and that you have spare batteries close at hand. If you plan to conduct a question and answer session with a large audience, arrange to have a microphone in the aisle for clients who wish to ask questions.
- ❍ Have your assistant sit at the entrance to your room at a formal registration desk. Provide her with a registration book and a sign that says, "Register here."

WIN SUCCESS WITH EXCITING DOOR PRIZES

What type of door prize would draw you to an event? Do your clients deserve anything less? As we have seen in discussing referral contests, whatever money you invest in quality door prizes is likely to be rewarded with valuable referrals. You must provide prizes that will be received enthusiastically. Two of the best seats in the house for the hottest show, best sporting event, or the finest restaurant are possibilities. Book the seats well in advance.

Let each of your guests know that there are two ways to win door prizes. The grand prize is reserved for the client who brings the largest number of guests to the event. Other clients and their guests can win by entering the draw when they arrive at the event. As you describe the prizes to your clients, ***sell them, don't tell them.*** Convince them that winning your grand prize will be the best thing that's happened to them all year!

As your clients and their guests arrive, have them register their names and addresses. Have your assistant record which guests attend with each client, and give everybody attending a draw ticket. At the same time, you should be welcoming each of your guests. Make each one feel like the most important person in the room. They just might be.

Once everyone is registered, have your assistant tally the number of guests and identify the client who has brought the greatest number of guests. You will announce this grand prize winner at the very end of the event.

FOLLOWING UP: TURNING GUESTS INTO CLIENTS

So far, you have held a wonderfully successful Client Appreciation Night. Your clients have arrived with guests in tow. Your presentation and refreshments have been well received. The grand prize winners were thrilled, and door prize winners are smiling all around the room. It's time now to turn all this happiness into business.

As the event draws to a close, distribute an appointment card that asks for the following information from each of your guests:

- ❍ Name, address, home and business phone numbers
- ❍ Best time to call
- ❍ Name of the person who referred them
- ❍ Products or services of interest
- ❍ Why is it important to act now instead of waiting?

You will also ask your guests to complete a feedback form. This form asks them to answer a series of positively framed questions about the evening, and to include their name and phone number. Collect the appointment and feedback forms before you announce the grand prize winner.

Immediately following the event, go through these forms. They represent the return on your investment in the event. Some guests will have said that they want to book an appointment with you immediately. Call them. Some will be 'fence-sitters.' Call them within twenty-four hours of the event, while the positive glow lingers. Use your best sales skills to turn them into clients and sources of more referrals!

COMMUNITY SPONSORSHIP: TURN GOOD WORKS INTO REFERRALS

Community sponsorships offer professionals and entrepreneurs a chance to develop strong, lasting relationships with their communities. With the right kind of involvement, these relationships can present you with many opportunities to drum up referrals. The cheque you write as a sponsor will be an investment in the well being of your community and in the chance to turn community feeling into referrals for your business.

How do you get started? I believe that you will excel if you find a group in need of financial support who is doing something that you love. In the long run, you may find that you can build your client base further with a different activity. But why not begin where your heart is? The advantages of sponsoring activities you love are clear. You get to spend working time at events that you enjoy. Your enjoyment will become part of your relationship with everyone involved in the activity. As you spend time with the group of people involved in your team or group, you will be able to offer knowledgeable praise for their achievements. They will appreciate your enthusiasm and moral support. You will be building an incredibly positive context for any business that results.

RECOGNIZE THE CENTRES OF INFLUENCE

When you attend games or events, try to locate the key people who influence the behaviour, beliefs and attitudes of others. These centres of influences exercise a kind of charisma. They are not always the wealthiest or best-educated people in the group. There may be several within the group you sponsor; many organizations are divided into a number of smaller groups based on background, interests or neighbourhood. As you spend time chatting with the key people in each group, everyone will begin to feel more comfortable associating with you. This comfort is essential if people are to approach you to do business with them.

BUILD TRUST BY TAKING BUSINESS TO YOUR OFFICE

For many years now, I have sponsored rep hockey teams in a small city about twenty minutes north of my home. When someone approaches me about financial products or insurance, I ask them to call me at my office. Over time, this has meant that people are more willing to do business with me. On the one hand, they know that I am concerned about protecting their privacy when we do business. On the other, they know that conversations with me do not necessarily end with a sales presentation. This reassurance makes it much easier for them to enjoy my company as we cheer on their children.

When prospects do approach you about business, you may wish to introduce a brief, non-threatening qualifying presentation. For instance, if someone asks you about insurance while you are at a game or event, you may respond: "Tell me why it is important for you to talk to me about insurance now, instead of six months or a year from now?"

This approach:

- overcomes the fear that you will push too hard or too quickly for a sale
- makes clients pre-handle their own objections by selling themselves on the need to do business
- avoids stalled appointments, because clients convince themselves that they should see you as soon as possible.

When you handle prospects in this way, you turn them into well-qualified potential clients before they step into your place of business.

A CHECKLIST FOR MAKING THE MOST OF YOUR SPONSORSHIPS

1 Find a team or group who need support and who are doing something you love.

2 Introduce yourself to the coaches or leaders. Make sure that you attend meetings with parents or participants and are introduced as a sponsor.

3 Become a presence. Attend games or events. Talk to the participants. Offer moral support. Where appropriate, provide refreshments or extras occasionally. Let the participants and volunteer leaders feel that you appreciate their efforts.

4 Don't talk shop at events. When approached, ask people to call you at your office. Let them know that they can approach you without exposing themselves to a "hard sell."

5 Locate the "centres of influence" among parents. Spend time at each event with these key people.

6 Create a brief, non-threatening qualifying presentation for use at events or games.

7 Plan newspaper advertising to appear at same time as articles on team achievements or special events.

COULD YOU PUT YOUR CLIENTS ON NATIONAL TELEVISION?

When you follow the practices I have outlined, you can be sure that your community sponsorships will become opportunities to drum up many referrals. You may also find that they offer opportunities to develop client relationships in surprising ways. Let me tell you about my most exciting experience as a community sponsor.

> After I had been a sponsor for several years, a Bantam Rep team with which I was involved was invited to participate in the Bobby Orr Easter Seals Hockey Tournament in Parry Sound. I decided to go with the team, but my car had other ideas. The Thursday I was to leave, it broke down.
>
> Instead of cancelling my trip, I asked a family if I could go with them. Bob and Ruth Craig had been my clients for several years. Their son, Andrew, was a top-notch goalie on the team I was sponsoring. The Craigs agreed to drive me and we set off for Parry Sound. When we arrived, I went to register and pay our tournament fees. The convenor invited me, as a sponsor, to have my picture taken with Don Cherry and Bobby Orr. After some persuasion, they agreed that the Craigs could come, too. We were the first people in the lounge.
>
> My eyes were immediately drawn to what I assumed was an excellent replica of the Stanley Cup. While we waited, I picked the cup up and lived the fantasy of holding it high over my head. Just at that moment, the convenor returned. "I saw that!" she laughed. I asked her where they had gotten the replica. "That's no replica," she said. "That's the real Stanley Cup." When I wondered where the security guards were to protect it, she explained, "Bobby arranges for the Hockey Hall of Fame to lend us the Cup every year. If that Cup went one foot out of this arena, the whole town would come together. I promise you, it would not go far."

> At that point, a line formed and we took our turn having our pictures taken with Don Cherry, Bobby Orr, and the Stanley Cup. Ruth Craig had come into the room with a Maple Leafs sweater over her arm. It had Felix Potvin's name on it. When Bobby Orr saw this, he had the photographer take a picture with the Potvin sweater held up in front of Ruth. What none of us realized at the time was that a CBC cameraman was filming the photo shoot. On Saturday night, the players and their parents gathered to watch the hockey game. Who should be featured on Coach's Corner that night but Ruth Craig, having her picture taken? My sponsorship had given a hockey mom - and a client - the thrill of a lifetime.

Ruth Craig is not only my client and my friend. She is a valuable centre of influence who has given me many referrals within her community. While you may not be able to put every client on national television, you can build strong and profitable relationships through sponsorships.

Sponsorships have given me many opportunities to do business. They have leveraged the paid advertising I do with invaluable publicity for team achievements and events. They have brought me many fine, long-term clients. More than this, they have made me a part of the communities where I do business. And they have given me countless "working" hours of real enjoyment. I encourage you to explore the power of community sponsorships. Like me, you will find that good quality sponsorships are a chance to have fun, drum up referrals, and truly touch the lives of many people.

CHAPTER SEVEN:

HAVE THE SUCCESS YOU IMAGINE

You now have all the strategies and tools you will need to drum up referrals. The only thing that could possibly stand between you and unlimited success is your own willingness to accept limitation. You may not yet be mentally prepared to accept your own success. You can change that.

This chapter presents ways of making you adopt more positive feelings about yourself and your work. You will come to believe that you deserve both the respect of your clients and their help in developing your business. This confidence will be strengthened as you create your own circle of excellence (a metaphor which usefully replaces the 'comfort zone'), and practice other visualization and affirmation techniques. You will convince yourself that you can drum up more referrals than you used to think possible.

Motivational tapes and books are a good beginning. Their creators provide you with the inspiration and the knowledge you need to move forward. You will continue to develop these qualities in yourself as you learn to recognize the state of mind required to ensure success. Finally, setting goals and timelines will get you ready to prepare and practice your delivery of referral presentations.

AFFIRMATIONS: TELLING YOURSELF THAT YOU WILL SUCCEED

In the first chapter of this book, we talked about the negative statements that we so often hear running through our heads. As we develop new presentation skills, we also need to change what our inner voices are telling us. We can do this by making regular use of affirmations.

Affirmations are statements we make that declare that we will achieve specific goals. They usually begin with the word "I" and include the positive end result for which we are striving. These statements are repeated over and over, either out loud or using our inner voices. The repetition continues until the end results are achieved. This kind of affirmation is well known and well documented. It offers a good start to mental preparation for getting more referrals.

We can, however, get even better results when we make use of the insight I will now share with you. The insight belongs to a brilliant psychiatrist and teacher named Dr. Uma Prasada. In the mid to late eighties, I had the privilege of studying psychology and psychiatry with Dr. Prasada. Along with our studies of famous thinkers and psychiatric disorders, we studied popular psychology. I was already familiar with the concepts of visualization and affirmation. But Dr. Prasada provided me with the 'missing link' that makes affirmations more effective in producing real-world successes.

According to Dr. Prasada, affirmations are most effective when practiced in three forms. Most people practice only the first form: They phrase their affirmations as statements beginning with "I" (first person). But to be really effective, affirmations should also be phrased as "You" (2nd person) and as "They" (3rd person) statements. Affirmations that are repeated regularly in all three forms are most likely to produce the results you want.

For example, you could use this set of three affirmations of your ability to drum up referrals. Repeat all three statements several times a day. In the first statement, imagine yourself speaking. In the second, imagine that someone significant to you is speaking to you. In the third, imagine that two people of significance to you are speaking to each other (about you).

1 "I drum up great referrals to my client base every day, and I enjoy the process."

2 "[Your name], your ability to drum up great referrals to your client base is incredible. You're the best at getting referrals!"

3 "[Your name] has been incredibly successful at drumming up great referrals to his/her client base. I'm very proud of him/her."

"Yes, and so you should be. [Your name] has gone above and beyond the call of duty and broken every record. He/She is guaranteed to win the referral contest!"

To get the 'biggest bang for your buck' when practicing affirmations, you must use all three forms: First, Second and Third Person!

CREATING YOUR OWN AFFIRMATIONS

It is time for you to make your own personal affirmations. Choose a particular goal you want to achieve. Then create affirmations in the first, second, and third person to help you achieve this goal.

First Person ("I"):

Second Person ("You"):

Third Person ("They"):

Congratulations - these affirmations will be an important step on your path to getting more referrals and earning greater success.

THE TRIANGLE OF CONFIDENCE: THREE WAYS TO FEEL TERRIFIC

Affirmations make you feel more confident about your own abilities. To design the right affirmations, you may have to ask questions about yourself, your skill level, the people with whom you work, and the company for which you work. You may be working independently (without a manager) or you may be self-employed (without either manager or company). The point is that you must have confidence in all aspects of your professional life and relationship with your clients.

The "Triangle of Confidence" is a strategy designed to help salespeople get a "lock" on their self-confidence. The triangle of confidence includes: feeling good about yourself; feeling good about your manager; feeling good about your company. By creating these three levels of confidence (before a presentation to a client is ever made), you strengthen your resistance to the anxiety you may feel when you think about the possibility of rejection.

On the other hand, when you are fully confident on all levels, you make it very easy for the client to buy into the presentation (because you "bought in" first). Credibility flows from the salesperson to the client, making rejection unlikely.

If you are not sure that you are currently feeling good about yourself, your manager, or your company, try these suggestions:

5 Ways to Feel Good About Yourself

1 Write a list of 10 qualities that make you a unique person, eg. I am honest, caring, punctual, loyal, etc.

2 Write a list of 50 things that you set out to achieve and did achieve.

3 Write a description of the attributes you currently possess which will make you an exceptional salesperson.

4 Write a detailed account of the successful life you have lived, as if you have already lived to a very old age.

5 Write your list of short, medium, and long-term goals (at least 50 goals in each category).

5 Ways to Feel Good about Your Manager

1 Write a list of the attributes you most respect and admire that your manager currently possesses.

2 Write a list of 20 different ways your manager has helped you in the past year.

3 Write a detailed account of the ideal relationship that could exist between you and your manager, then work toward creating that relationship.

4 Write a list of the strengths your manager possesses that you are not currently using.

5 Write a list of objectives (that no other salesperson would bother with) that you could help your manager achieve.

5 Ways to Feel Good about Your Company

1 Write a list of all the reasons that you went to work for the company.

2 Write out the company's mission statement and a detailed account of how that mission statement is in keeping with your core values and beliefs-and your ability to earn referrals.

3 Write a list of all the benefits you receive for working for this company.

4 Write a "recruiting presentation." In other words, write out a script that you would use if you were "enticing" someone to come to work with you and your company.

5 Gather the Annual Reports from the past 5 years,

and document the positive progress the company has made as it relates to you and your customers.

Remember:
A Triangle Must Always Have 3 Sides

Perhaps you have carefully considered all the questions suggested above, and you still have trouble feeling good about one side of your triangle. Is it possible to drum up referrals if you are missing one or more sides of your triangle of confidence?

What if you do not feel good about you? Simply put, if you do not feel good about yourself, how could you ever possibly get a potential client to feel good about you, or your products and services? How could a client refer his or her friends to you?

You must take responsibility for feeling good about yourself. Take action. If you don't, who will?

What happens if you do not feel good about your manager? Generally, if you do not have a good relationship with your manager you may have less support than you need, and you will almost certainly have to cope with negative attitudes at work (and maybe in other places, too):

❍ You might not ask for the help you need.

❍ You might misinterpret your manager's positive suggestions.

❍ You might engage in "avoidance behaviours." These behaviours might be interpreted as laziness or bad attitude by other managers. As a result, you may be 'overlooked' at promotion time.

- ❍ You might carry negative emotional baggage into other areas of your life.
- ❍ You might subconsciously blow a big sale because you resent the large overwrite in commission that your manager would make.

TAKE RESPONSIBILITY FOR COMMUNICATING YOUR EXPECTATIONS TO YOUR MANAGER. WORK OUT AN ACTION PLAN THAT WILL SATISFY YOU-AND YOUR MANAGER!

What happens if you do not feel good about your company? In today's fiercely competitive market, most salaried employees are all too willing to accept the negatives of working for a company, even if those negatives are in direct violation of their personal belief systems or core values. If you are legitimately conflicted about the company you represent, you will not be able to achieve personal satisfaction and create an environment where clients send you an endless stream of referrals.

IF YOU DO NOT FEEL GOOD ABOUT YOUR COMPANY - TAKE MASSIVE ACTION TOWARD FINDING A COMPANY THAT WILL SUPPORT YOUR BELIEFS AND VALUES. THEN QUIT! GO TO WORK FOR THAT COMPANY. DEDICATE YOUR WORKING HOURS TO SUPPORTING YOUR NEW COMPANY'S MISSION STATEMENT. YOU WILL ENJOY BEING "ON PURPOSE" WITH YOUR WORK AND YOUR LIFE.

VISUALIZING YOUR SUCCESS

Visualization is a process of creating an image on the screen of your mind. The image can be anything you want it to be. It can be black and white or color, moving or stationary, bright or dark. You can see yourself in the picture, or you can see the picture as if you were looking through your own eyes. Once you get the hang of visualization, you can see yourself being as successful as you like. See yourself getting more referrals than ever before. See these referrals lining up at your door. See them signing huge cheques made out to your company. See them giving you more referrals than you ever thought possible. Such images are more than wishful thinking. They are the first step in reaching the success you imagine.

For example, try this. Imagine that you are sitting at an awards banquet. When you look around, you see the most important people in your life. They are all impressively dressed in their finest clothes. They are seated at banquet tables. On the tables are programs. When you look at one of these programs, you notice the category "National Referral Champion." Under this category, ***you see your own name.*** You watch the Master of Ceremonies step up to the microphone. He introduces you as this year's most outstanding referral champion, and invites you to accept a brightly polished trophy. As you accept the award, the audience rises to their feet in a standing ovation.

IF YOU CAN SEE IT HAPPEN,
YOU CAN MAKE IT HAPPEN.

Just as your subconscious mind stores the messages on motivational tapes, it stores the messages you send it through visualization. When you visualize your own success, you take a step towards believing that such success is possible. This confidence, in turn, will allow you to behave in ways that ensure your success will become real.

EXERCISE YOUR VISUALIZATION "MUSCLES"

Some people have difficulty with visualization. As much as they would like to "see" themselves succeed, they find that their minds just don't work this way. They have enough trouble visualizing familiar faces, telephone numbers, or the new outfit they bought last week. Maybe you remember sounds, tastes, or movements more easily than you remember images. You may need to tone up your visualization "muscles" before using this technique to prepare for your success. The exercises that follow are designed to improve your ability to visualize:

1 Look around the room in which you are sitting. Stare at a series of objects located in the room. Once you have a picture of those objects firmly in your mind, close your eyes. With your eyes closed, recreate the picture of the objects on the screen of your mind. When you have had a good "look" around this visualization of your room, open your eyes. How many objects were you able to include?

2 Take a look around the room in which you are sitting. Identify all the objects that are brown. Then, close your eyes and create a visual image on

the screen of your mind. Include all the brown objects. If you feel confident that you have been able to visualize all the brown objects, keep your eyes closed. Look around your visualization of the room again. How many blue objects can you see this time?

3 Take a good long look at the following list of numbers and letters. When you feel you know the list, close your eyes. Recreate the list in your mind's eye. When you can see it clearly (while keeping your eyes closed), recite the list into a tape recorder. Then open your eyes, and play back the tape to see how successful you were.

48get8e9lots653687of54698216referrals854uhphhp786i6

4 With the help of a partner and a dictionary of difficult or unusual words, you can improve your ability to both visualize and speller - I mean spell. Ask your partner to open the dictionary to any page and select a difficult word. Ask your partner to say the word out loud twice: first, correctly, and then phonetically. Your challenge is to first visualize the word, then spell it correctly.

If you repeat these exercises over several weeks, or even months, you will notice a dramatic improvement in your ability to visualize - and win spelling bees.

THE CIRCLE OF EXCELLENCE

Once you are comfortable with your ability to visualize, you are ready to expand your sales potential. Visualization will allow you to replace your current "comfort zone" with a "circle of excellence." The circle of excellence creates the most effective mindset for selling and attaining optimal results.

Your comfort zone is a metaphor for the limits you are currently putting on your own ability to succeed. Outside the comfort zone lies (yes, I mean "lies") a zone that you perceive as dangerous. This perception will often prevent you from extending the limit of your sales potential.

In the past, you might have been encouraged to try to expand your comfort zone. You probably would not have succeeded. When you continually push against the limits of your comfort zone, your natural mechanisms "kick in" to try to make you more comfortable again. This conflict is likely to override both your good intentions and Management by Objectives.[2]

It is more effective to replace the "comfort zone" metaphor with a better one, than to try to expand it. Here is a method for visualizing a "Circle of Excellence" that can prepare you for unlimited success:

1. Visualize a circle approximately 3 feet in diameter on the floor in front of you.

2. Visualize the circle filled with a foundation of bright gold.

3 Remember and visualize a time when you were completely successful.

4 Place this experience in the centre of the circle.

5 Repeat steps 3 and 4 many times, vividly recalling and reliving each experience.

6 Step into the circle and feel the way you felt during each experience of success.

7 Repeat the process until the circle of excellence is hard-wired into your personal psychology.

8 Repeat steps 1 through 7 in preparation for each and every sales call.

9 Continually expand the circle of excellence by adding each and every new achievement to the circle. Place each achievement in the circle as soon as possible after you experience it.

SEE AND SAY TO SUCCEED!

To be as successful as possible, you need to match visualizations with affirmations. This is called "coupling." Coupling or joining affirmations with visualizations gives you the most effective mental preparation for success. How do I know? Let me tell you how the combination of affirmation and visualization led me to outstanding success in the first two months of my career as a financial planner.

> From 1976 until 1987, I had the good fortune to have Gabor Szekely as my Financial Planner. Every time I went to Gabor's office, I saw a beautiful brass plaque on his wall, "The Master Millionaire Award." The inscription on

[2]Management by objectives is a method for setting performance standards as they relate to the objectives one is expected to achieve, usually in business.

the plaque read: "In recognition of outstanding achievement with personal sales volume in excess of $3,000,000 in one year." Gabor had won the award every year, ten years in a row.

During the summer of 1987, Gabor introduced me to a career in Financial Planning with "Investors Group Financial Services, Inc.," the company for which he worked. At this point, my only knowledge of financial planning was what I had learned from Gabor while I was his client. My official start date with Investors was Monday, October 26, 1987 - one week after Black Monday, the big stock market crash.

By the second week, referrals were pouring in, and I set my sights on the "Master Millionaire Award." I wanted to win this award by December 31, 1987—only two months away. During my first month, I earned $35,000, but when I asked for information on the possibility of winning the award in such a short time, I was told, "It can't be done. No one has done it before!" People laughed at me behind my back and they laughed at me to my face. By now, you've probably guessed that I did win the award in the last two months of 1987. I also caught and passed the top rookie in the office to win the title, "Rookie of the Year."

As a result of my achievement (driven by the strategies that you have been learning throughout this book), Bill Roth, the Investors' Group Regional Vice-President for Ontario, asked me to be a keynote speaker at the company's 1988 convention. Bill asked me to talk about the success I created in my first two months as a financial planner. I agreed, but asked to get back to him about the title of my talk. I did not know what to call it.

When I asked my friend, Dr. Prasada, she suggested that I talk about using visualization and affirmation together. This strategy had been the single most important factor

> in my success. The title of the talk almost became the term we used to describe the combination of visualization and affirmation in my psychology lessons: "Coupling." We knew what coupling meant.
>
> To his credit, Bill Roth strongly suggested that I choose another title. Could you imagine the disappointment on the faces of people coming to hear a talk on "coupling," only to be sold on the benefits of practicing and perfecting the craft of visualization and affirmation?

You, of course, know better than those conference goers. So, let's look at how 'coupling' can help you drum up referrals.

CREATING PERFECT COUPLES

Simply put, to create a perfect couple you need to combine a visual image of success with the affirmation that best represents the outcome you want. You can have different affirmations accompanying a single picture, or you can pair different pictures with a single affirmation. You can "see and say" in any way that focuses your commitment and improves your confidence.

Here is an example of a set of "couples" which might work for you. At the beginning of this book, I introduced you to the 'Essence of Success' as captured and defined by Doug Dawson. As you recall, Doug asserted that:

> "HIGH PERFORMERS TAKE CHARGE AND CAUSE RESULTS TO HAPPEN. THEY LEVERAGE UP OPPORTUNITY AND ASK FOR BUSINESS. THEY TURN A SATISFIED CUSTOMER INTO A REFERRAL. THEY MAKE THE TIME TO ACHIEVE SUCCESS."

Let's turn this assertion into 'couples' in the first, second and third person. Practice each 'couple' until you have fully internalized the process. It is important that you are able to recall and relive this visualization and affirmation whenever you wish.

First Person: Picture yourself sitting in a comfortable chair. Your head is held high. You have a triumphant smile on your face. You are absolutely bursting with pride as you take each deep breath. As you enjoy reliving this picture of success to its fullest, you hear yourself saying, "I am a high performer. I take charge and cause results to happen. I move beyond the transaction request. I leverage up opportunity and ask for the business. I turn satisfied customers into referrals. I make the time to achieve success."

Second Person: You are at the office. Your manager has just burst through the door with a huge grin on his face. He is flushed with excitement, and you can tell that he is about to say something very positive. Speaking at a speed and pitch that the 'Chipmunks' would envy, he says: "[Your name], you are a high performer who takes charge. You cause results to happen. You move beyond the transaction request. You leverage up opportunity and ask for the business. You turn satisfied customers into referrals. You make the time to achieve success. And these are only a few of the qualities I admire about you!"

Third Person: It's awards night at the office. Your boss and your boss's boss are standing off to one side of the trophy table. They are admiring the biggest trophy, a trophy with your name on it.

As you approach, you hear them saying: "[Your name] is a high performer who takes charge and causes results to happen. S/he moves beyond the transaction request. S/He leverages up opportunity and asks for the business. S/He turns a satisfied customer into a referral. Best of all, the quality I admire most about [your name] is that s/he takes the time to achieve success!"

Remember, when you combine visualizations and affirmations, your success will be determined by four things:

REPETITION AND CONTINUAL REFINEMENT

REPETITION AND CONTINUAL REFINEMENT

REPETITION AND CONTINUAL REFINEMENT

REPETITION AND CONTINUAL REFINEMENT

CONDITION YOURSELF TO SUCCEED

Using the same principles, you may put your sub-conscious to work for you in other ways, too. A famous philosopher once said: "We don't have habits, our habits have us." How many of your current habits are moving you closer to your goals? Investing in yourself to develop better attitudes and skills is a habit that will change the way you do business and help you to drum up referrals.

Consider one example from my own experience. Before I began my current career as a Financial Planner with the Investors Group, I taught "The Dale Carnegie Course in Effective Speaking and Human Relations." As part of my development in that role, I was required to listen to motivational tapes by a man named Zig Ziglar. The tapes were resources for quotations and anecdotes to enhance my teaching of the course. As the incident that follows demonstrates, they also became a permanent part of my way of thinking.

I immediately fell in love with the Zig Ziglar tapes, and invested in all the other tapes, books and video-cassettes sold through the Zig Ziglar Corporation. In particular, the "How to Stay Motivated" and "Secrets of Closing the Sale" tapes became my constant companions. I always played a motivational audio-cassette while I was in my car. Even when my mind seemed preoccupied by other things, a developmental tape was playing in the background.

Two years later, I was just winding up a successful financial planning appointment with a client. On a scale of 1 to 10, the appointment had definitely been a "9." I asked the client for a referral. The look on his face let me know right away that the request made him uncomfortable.

I asked the client why the request bothered him. He told me that, "I like you. I think you're a nice guy and a good financial planner. But you have not yet proven yourself. When I see some results, I'll recommend you to my friends."

When I asked what kind of results he needed, he went on: "It's not even the results I need to see. It's the details - I don't understand all the details. You've explained things very well, and I understand what you say when you say it. But what would happen if I recommended you to a friend and they asked me to explain the details? I would not be able to do it."

Instantly, I knew how to handle his objections. I asked him to explain how a farmer can feed his black cow green grass and then have that cow produce white milk, yellow butter, orange cheese and red meat. My client asked me to repeat the question. Then he asked, "What's a cow got to do with financial planning?"

I answered him with another question. Could he explain to me how a dark room is flooded with light from a bulb in the ceiling when you push a button the wall? He could not. Did he use wall switches to turn on the lights at his house? He did. "So," I concluded, "Even when we do not know the details of the things we enjoy, we can still enjoy their benefits? Can't we?"

He stared at me for what seemed like hours. Finally, he reached up to rub his chin, and a grin spread across his face. "I see what you mean." He went on to give me the names of two friends he thought should see me right away.

How did I know exactly what to say to save this situation and win the referrals I wanted? At first, I assumed that I was a "sales genius."

Two weeks later, I was driving along listening to Zig Ziglar's ***Secrets of Closing the Sale*** cassette. Guess what? My brilliant strategy for overcoming the "I need more details" objection was right there on the tape! I must have played that tape in my car at least a hundred times. Consciously, my mind was always somewhere else. I do not remember ever hearing that close before or making a conscious effort to memorize that strategy. And yet my subconscious mind must have picked that strategy off the tape and stored it.

Listening to motivational tapes had "programmed" me for success. And I had the referrals to prove it!

IS YOUR MIND CONDITIONED TO SUCCEED?

As you have seen, I was ready to respond to my client because I had made an investment in developing my knowledge and skills. Your investment in self-development is the first sign of a commitment to your own success.

Take a moment now to evaluate how much of a commitment you have made to self-development:

❍ Do you dedicate a portion of each day to reading a motivational book?

❍ Do you invest a portion of each day in listening to a motivational tape?

❍ Do you set aside a portion of each day for watching a motivational video?

❍ Do you attend motivational seminars on a regular basis?

❍ Do you read books on selling on a daily basis?

❍ Do you listen to tapes on selling on a daily basis?

❍ Do you watch videotapes about selling on a daily basis?

❍ Do you attend sales-training seminars on a regular basis?

- ❍ Do you write out and refine your sales presentation on a regular basis?
- ❍ Do you write out and review your goals on a regular basis?
- ❍ Do you have an action plan to improve your self-image?
- ❍ Do you have an exercise program that you do daily?

Review your responses. Is it possible that the habits listed above (all habits worth investing in) are now absent from your daily routine? Is the absence of one or more of these habits holding you back from achieving success? You won't know until you put these habits to work for you.

JUST DO IT!

Make time each day to invest in yourself. With time and repetition, you can develop habits that will put you well on the road to unlimited success.

CONGRUENCY: TOTALLY PREPARED FOR SELLING SUCCESS

Congruency is one of the key ingredients that separates the Sales Superstar from the "Sales Superstar Wanna-Be". When you have congruency, your mind, body and actions are in complete harmony. Congruency makes your sales message 100% believable.

How does congruency work? When you communicate a message, any message, the listener is judging you. S/he will be measuring the 'believability' of both the message and the messenger. When a listener detects mixed signals, s/he is less likely to believe in either the message or the messenger.

The state of sending such mixed messages is called incongruency. Consider, for instance, the conflicting messages sent by a bad salesperson. S/he tells you that this new and improved 'booshmenge-gizmo' is the greatest thing since sliced bread - but somehow, you don't believe it. Chances are, you are hearing a positive message and, at the same time, reading or interpreting the way the message is being delivered as negative. This is incongruency.

Congruency feels much better. To recreate your congruent state, recall a time when you got something you really wanted - an award, treat, present, or experience that you really looked forward to. As you relive that experience mentally, you will begin to recognize the feeling of total congruency. Can you find some internal feeling, sight, or sound that will unmistakably define congruency for you?

You may wonder how to move from this sense of congruency to the state of mind in which you normally deliver sales presentations. How can you make sure you have congruency when you talk to clients? Every section in the first four chapters of this book has been designed to help you improve your state of congruency.

You are now well on your way to both congruency and to getting more referrals. You have already taken these steps towards congruency:

- ❍ You use motivational tapes and other resources to develop your confidence and skills
- ❍ You feel good about yourself, your manager and your company
- ❍ You regularly practice affirmation and visualization
- ❍ You step into your circle of excellence before every sales presentation.

Mentally and emotionally, you are now prepared to meet clients with a congruent message. You know that you deserve success, and that soon your customers will know it too.

CONCLUSION:

THE ZEN OF ASKING FOR REFERRALS

Long ago there was a Zen master by the name of Wuhan.

Wuhan was humane and considerate, and he conducted himself with modesty and austerity.

Whenever he spoke, his words were simple yet the meaning was profound.

He studied widely and had a strong memory. He would pursue reason to its final conclusion, and did not stop on any account, or follow anything arbitrarily.

When he discussed a story, contemporary or ancient, it was like being there in person - to those who heard, it was as clear as seeing with their own eyes.

Students used to say that a year of meditation was not as good as a day of listening to the master's talk.

The Zen master's quiet talk seems to be completely different than the image of the drummer with which we started this book. It's not as different as it seems. Wuhan had attained a state of total congruence in which he was so completely in tune with himself and others that he attracted referrals. His quiet congruence attracted as much attention as the steady beating of a drum.

Let me share two more contemporary examples of total congruence at work. In both, professionals have built extremely successful businesses by committing themselves to developing great relationships with every one of their customers.

My parents, Tom and Elen, have life-long friends who own and operate a very successful art supply store in North Hollywood, California. The business is called World Supply Graphic Arts, and the owners are Murray and Geri Ross. One incident illustrates their dedication to the highest levels of customer satisfaction.

We were visiting the store on a family vacation. The store was very busy, and the order department had a problem. One of the local universities had placed an order that was required immediately. The university could not send anyone out to pick up the order, and the delivery personnel at World Supply were all busy. Murray's response was immediate and straightforward. He called the head of the Art Department at the University and told him that he would deliver the material himself.

Murray was supposed to be on holiday with us that week. He could have simply sent the material by courier. Instead, he demonstrated extraordinary concern with his clients' satisfaction. This concern has nurtured his business from its origins in the family garage to the super store it has become today.

Meanwhile, in Toronto another entrepreneur has been steadily growing his own business. Dave Hamilton owns a store called "Just Drums." For many years, I visited the store without making any significant purchases. Nonetheless, every time I walked into "Just Drums" Dave Hamilton made a point of making me feel very welcome. Clearly, he was ready to invest heavily in creating a long-term relationship with his customers. As a result, I recommended the store to many of my friends. When I finally purchased a new drum set recently, I bought it at Just Drums.

Practicing the attitudes, exercises and skills covered in this book will inevitably allow you to drum up referrals immediately. You will get referrals simply by asking for them, persistently and tactfully. However, if you really want to stretch the limits of your success, I encourage you to develop long-term, congruent relationships with each of your clients. In exceeding their expectations, you will show that you have become the kind of drummer who draws a crowd. You will drum up referrals and attract the business that leads to unlimited success.

APPENDIX I:
SAMPLE REFERRAL CARDS

What happens when a client agrees to give you referrals? If you can pull out a suitable referral card, it is easy to get all the information you need in a form that will make it easy to use, track or transcribe into your computer contact database. Feel free to photocopy, scan or reproduce the five cards that follow. Each will help you work with particular clients to increase their satisfaction and build your client base.

REFERRAL CARD 1

Use this card to drum up referrals from clients who are hesitant. Ask them to focus on the benefits that their friends or colleagues will derive from speaking with you. This card will help you get one or two names (that you might not get otherwise) and will reassure your client that he or she has made a good decision.

Name: ______________________________

Address: ______________________________

Phone Number: Res. ______________ Bus. ______________

Occupation: ______________________________

Relationship: ______________________________

Benefits: ______________________________

____

REFERRAL CARD 2

The drummer knows he has been successful when a crowd gathers around him. Some clients will be willing to reward your exceptional service and competence with a whole crowd of referrals. Use this card with clients who are eager to give you the names of several friends who will benefit from speaking with you. Don't be afraid to gather a crowd; they will reinforce one another's good judgement in dealing with you!

Name: ____________________

Phone: Res. __________ Bus. __________

Name: ____________________

Phone: Res. __________ Bus. __________

Name: ____________________

Phone: Res. __________ Bus. __________

Name: ____________________

Phone: Res. __________ Bus. __________

REFERRAL CARD 3

Use this card when you are working with clients who take special satisfaction in helping others. Often they are grandparents, older brothers or sisters, or firstborns.

These clients will be glad to help you drum up referrals, because they will also be helping the friends they refer to you. Talk with them about the many reasons their friends, family, or colleagues need your product or service. The more convinced they are, the more names they will offer. Equally important, as they talk about the benefits of doing business with you, they will increase their own satisfaction.

Whom Can I Help?

1 Name: ______________________
Phone:______________________
Why: ______________________

2 Name: ______________________
Phone:______________________
Why: ______________________

3 Name: ______________________
Phone:______________________
Why: ______________________

REFERRAL CARD 4

This card works well with clients who have a high need for the approval of others. It will be very important that these clients are sure that the people they refer will be happy to have the chance to do business with you.

Be careful not to use this card with anyone who might find the title corny. Cards are useful, but the heart of drumming up referrals is your relationship with your clients.

Happily Referred Friends

Name: ______________________________

Address: ______________________________

Phone: ______________________________

Occupation: ______________________________

Basis of Friendship: ______________________________

Reasons for Referring: ______________________________

____

____

REFERRAL CARD 5

People like people who are like themselves. If your client will only give you one name, try this card. Your client's best friend probably needs to do business with you.

My Best Friend

Name: ____________ Address: ____________

Phone: Res. ____________ Bus. ____________

Occupation: ____________ Company: ____________

Approx. Salary: ____________ Approx. Net Worth: ____________

Age: ____________ Homeowner? ❑ Yes ❑ No

Married? ❑ Yes ❑ No Dependents? ❑ Yes ❑ No

Best Time to Call: ❑ AM ❑ PM Hobbies: ____________

Reason for Referring? ____________

APPENDIX II:

DAN BODANIS, CAREER HIGHLIGHTS

ABOUT THE AUTHOR:

Dan Bodanis has helped thousands of sales professionals to drum up the referrals they need. His seminar, "Drumming Up Referrals" prepares participants to ask for, and get as much new business as they can handle. Dan's motivational speaking, workshops, and one on one sales training inspire others to develop high quality client relationships.

For almost 15 years Dan was a leading consultant with Canada's largest financial planning company. He has also been a National Sales Leader with two different Life Insurance companies. His background includes training, speaking, writing and an active and successful career as a studio musician and teacher of drumming.

Dan supports every seminar with a workbook and follow-up program. From Dan's perspective, the greatest complement he can receive is your repeat business and a gift of many referrals.

Would you like Dan to inspire and guide your sales force? He will work with you to ensure that his seminar is customized to meet your unique needs. Contact Dan for a presentation that marches to your beat!

www.danbodanis.com

WOULD YOU LIKE TO INVEST A GREAT DEAL MORE IN THE PEOPLE THAT WORK WITH YOU AND AROUND YOU?

If you are interested in purchasing this book for your sales force, department, or company, please contact Dan Bodanis.

Discounts for purchases of multiple copies will apply as follows:

30 - 99 copies	5% discount
100 - 249 copies	10% discount
250 - 499 copies	15% discount
500 - 749 copies	20% discount
749 - 1000 copies	25% discount

Contact Dan Bodanis to arrange a discount or customized services for orders of more than 1000 copies.

www.danbodanis.com

ABOUT THE ARTIST:

Lar deSouza is a humourous illustrator and caricaturist who is skilled in both traditional and digital media. He has done projects ranging from desktop publishing and advertising to interactive software as well as commissions for individuals.

Lar deSouza may be reached at:

LAR DESOUZA

4 DIVISION STREET

ACTON ON L7J 1C3

TELEPHONE: 519-853-5819

EMAIL: FRESCO@SENTEX.NET

PRINTING AND COVER DESIGN BY:

Central is much more than a printing company, offering a wide range of solutions for the corporate marketplace.

We offer eye-catching designs, quick processing of client disks, high-quality proofs, photo scanning and retouching, large format posters, and the latest technology to go directly from computer to press plate.

Our presses can handle anything from one-colour letterhead to five-colour catalogues, while our Xerox department provides instant printing and colour copies.

A full bindery department finishes your job, and our mailing department can imprint addresses from your database. We offer warehouse services and ship products across North America.

This total approach allows us to deliver top quality, while saving our customers both time and money.

CENTRAL REPRODUCTIONS LTD.
4524 EASTGATE PARKWAY
MISSISSAUGA, ON L4W 3W6
TELEPHONE: 905-238-1250
FAX: 905-238-4994
Website: www.central-repro.com

Central
REPRODUCTIONS LTD.

SteakFrites, 692 Mount Pleasant Rd. 416-486-0090
Oliver and Bonacini Café, Grill Bayview Village Shopping Centre,
2901 Bayview Ave. 416-590-1300
Lucy's Seafood, 6905 Millcreek Drive,
Len, Lucy, or Peter 905-567-8950
3145 Dundas St., Mississauga 905-569-3656
North 44 Restaurant, 2537 Yonge St. 416-487-4897
www.north44restaurant.com north.44@rogers.com
Via Allegro Trattoria, 1750 The Queensway, Etobicoke 416-622-6677
EDO, 484 Eglington Ave. West 416-322-3033
EDO-ko, 431 Spadina Rd. 416-482-8973
di.ferent by EDO, 257 Adelaide St. West 416-977-8744
EDO Delivery 416-322-8888
Millers Country Fare Restaurants Ltd. 5140 Dundas St. West, Islington
George McDonald 416-234-5050
La Sem Ristorante, 1275 Eglinton Ave. E., Mississauga 905-624-8888
Camarra Pizzeria Ristorante, 2899 Dufferin St., Toronto 416-789-3221
LE PAPILLON, 16 Church Street 416-363-0838
Inn on the Twenty, 905-562-5336
3836 Main St., Jordon, Ont., www.innonthetwenety.com

Toronto Jazz Clubs

Montreal Bistro & Jazz Club, 65 Sherbourne St. 416-363-0179
www.montrealbistro.com
Top of the Senator, 253 Victoria St. 416-364-7517
The Rex Hotel, 194 Queen St. West 416-598-2475

Great Ice Cream and More!

Caffé Demetre Amazing Desserts and Great Homemade Ice Cream
Tony, Louie or Helen 905-829-2400
La Paloma Gelateria & Café Carmelo Giannone 416-656-2340
or 905-851-5151
Opera Emporium (Gemstones & Ice Cream), Tom Knott 905-854-5106

The Village of Elora

Grand Gourmet, 42 West Mill Street, Elora, Ontario 519-846-5771
Sharon Scott, Prop.
The Elora Mill, 77 West Mill Street, Elora, Ontario
Phone Jennifer Smith, Innkeeper 519-846-9118
information@eloramill.com www.eloramill.com/
Elora General Store, 15 Mill Street East, Elora, Ontario 519-846-2600
Rhoda Lipton, Barbara Lee, Prop. info@eloragenerалstore.com
www.elorageneralstore.com
Let It Bee, Located in The Elora Mews - Shops by the Elora Gorge
45 West Mill Street, Elora, Ontario 519-846-5733
Richelle Monaghan info@letitbee.com www.letitbee.com
Serendipity Restaurant, Jason Pilkington, 13 East Mill St., Elora 519-846-8738
Night & Day Studio, 11 Mill Street East, Elora, Ontario 519-846-9222
Elsa Mann, night_day_studio@hotmail.com

Chiropractors:

Dr. Pat Hewitt, www.docwellness.com or 905-820-4620
Dr. Joe Hewitt 905-820-4620
Dr. Mark Fleet, markev@istar.ca or 905-338-1986
Dr. Pavit Kapoor 905-338-1548
Dr. Dev Sarathy, dr.dev@rogers.com 905-820-4620

Dr. Nancy Korenic, nkorenic@yahoo.com 905-820-4620 or 416-275-7387
Dr. Don Rogers 905-820-4620
Dr. Mike Pangelinan, Hollywood California - Chiropractic & AK. 818-792-0998
www.ucmg.net

Animal Chiropractor

Dr. Susanne Langdon , sjrooster@aol.com 1-905-468-1066

Athletic Therapy, Massage, Acupuncture & Shiatsu

Alberto Gregori, 905-873-2361, 905-846-2020
Don Norton, RMT Massage Therapy 905-867-0594
Shiatsu and Japanese Massage, Yaz Yamaguchi 416-892-1279
Presence Acupuncture and Shiatsu Clinic, Masami or Sara 416-484-0486

Osteopath

Dr. Glen Sprague, Ontario Osteopathic and Rehabilitation Clinic 905-335-5533

Orthotics

Footmaxx, Leanne Simons, Manager, Marketing and Education 416-366-3668
or 1-800-779-3668 ext. 228

Naturopathic Doctors

Dr. Cathy Kuindersma 905-873-2361
Dr. Ann Nakajima 905-338-1548

Reiki Master

Florine Phillips, Personal Touch Holistic Services, Holistic Practitioner
personaltouch54@hotmail.com 905-339-2477

Meditation and Eastern Philosophy Instruction

Tony Murdock, Meditation Instructor 905-820-5470
www.towardstillness.com
Heather Murdock, Yoga Instructor 905-820-5470
Toney Philadelphia, Private Fitness and Martial Arts Instruction 905-272-3338

Hearing Clinic

Plimmer Hearing Centre 905-607-2022

Optometrist

Dr Martin Traynor, Sherway Gardens Mall 416-695-8206

Opticians

Illuminata Eyewear, Tenny Tsang 416-620-8028

Real Estate and Home Related Services

Mary Henderson 416-236-6000
www.maryhenderson@trebnet.com or www.maryhendersonhomes.com
Debbie Pearce 905-320-9484, 905-690-2666
Earl McCallum, www.earlmccallum.com 905-568-2121
Steven Dao, stevendaok@hotmail.com 905-279-8300
Gabe Kim, www.gabekim.com or gabekim@canada.com 416-582-9666
Ian R. Dance, idance@trebnet.com 905-822-6900
Feng Shui Specialist/Consultant - Steven Dao 905-279-8300
Home and Commercial Security - System Advisors ADT, Carl Attim 416-892-1050
Carrier Heating and Air Conditioning, www.carrier.com 1-800-4Carrier
Maidday Home Cleaning Services, Jayce King, President 1-888-624-3329

Lawyers

Andrew Buckstein, Hoffman Silary Buckstein and Chuback 416-787-1161
www.abuckstein@hsbclaw.com ext.223
William R. Gale, Grosman, Grosman & Gale, www.grosman.com 416-364-9599
Stan Fisher, Heenan Blaikie LLP, www.heenanblaikie.com 416-360-6336
Lara Edwards, Heenan Blaikie LLP, www.heenanblaikie.com 416-360-6336

Accountant
John McCormick 905-257-1550

Bookkeeping
Bronte Bookkeeping, Susan Pink 905-849-4300

Actuarial Consultant & Estate Planning Specialist
Cliff Oliver 416-258-9992

Pension Specialist
Gilles R. Marceau and Associates 416-986-2015

Venture Capital/Corporate Finance
Andy Gravitis, agravitis1@cogeco.ca 905-339-2473

Car Companies
Mercedes Benz Retail Sales, Donna Van De Beek 416-255-1132, ext: 241
vandebeek@mercedes-benz.ca
Lexus of Oakville, Frank Apa 905-847-8400
frank@lexusofoakville.ca or www.lexusofoakville.com
Oakville Toyota, Frank Apa 905-842-8400
frank@oakvilletoyota.ca or www.oakvilletoyota.ca
GM Automobiles, Highland Chev-Olds - Cadillac, Garry Sleep 905-727-9444,
garry@highlandgm.com
Oakville Honda, James Shin, General Sales Manager 905-844-9831
Lexus of Richmond Hill, Spencer Morgan, 905-883-8812
647-293-0337, spencerm@lexusrh.com
Chrysler Automobiles, Cooksville Chrysler, Sean Kelly 905-279-3031
www.cooksvilledodge.com
Wholesale Dealers Network Dennis Downey CFO 1-613-843-8656
ddowney@wholesaledealersnetwork.com

Men's Clothes
Jonathon Quinn Men's Wear - Joe or Natasha 905-820-3317
Harry Rosen Men's Wear www.harryrosen.com
Perry's Vern Riediger 416-923-7397

Personal Shopping Services/Men's Clothing Consultant
Charles D. Waterman 416-720-0665

Music Services
Tommy Bodanis Band 416-247-8014
The Dan Bodanis Band 905-609-2515
Tony Padalino Recording Studio www.tonypadalino.com
tonypadalino@tonlinproductions.com
Linda Cara, Vocal Instruction www.TonLinproductions.com
Grant Avenue Studio, Bob Doidge or Paul Reimens 905-522-5227
Merriam School of Music, www.merriammusic.com 905-829-2020
Toronto Musicians Association, Bill Skolnik 416-420-1020
www.torontomusicians.org
Tony Mergel Music Productions 905-819-8766
Bandwagon Event Production, Bill Lutes, blutes3@cogeco.ca 905-549-2732
Tom Skublics Musical Entertainment, skublics@ica.net 905-826-4042
The Chris John Show, www.chrisjohnshow.com
Swing Low Productions Inc., Orin Isaacs, orin@mocamusic.com 416-410-0869
First Bass Music, Andrew Buntain 416-898-6348
andrew@firstbassmusic.com www.firstbassmusic.com
Downstroke, Perry Busch, www.downstoke.ca 416-420-1500
Al Hirsch Music Services, hirsmusic@rogers.com 905-274-4140
The Al Henderson Quintet 416-503-3866
and Time Warp www.cornerstonerecords.com
Neil Christoffersen, christof@spectranet.ca 905-827-8186

The Dave Field Band 905-822-7534
The Eric Boucher Band 416-698-7983
Silard Somorjay, Master of the Grand Piano, www.silardsomorjay.com 1-702-250-2967
Levon Ichkanian, International Award Winning Guitarist, www.levonmusic.com
Drummers Choice Drum Store, David Harvey 905-455-9884

Drum Teachers

Jeff Salem, www.salemdrum.com 416-564-9802
Marc Atkinson, Las Vegas Nevada zatkinson@lvcm.com
Dom Famularo www.domfamularo.com

Hotels

Holiday Inn Select Airport 416-798-5809
Brian Dec, Director of Sales and Marketing, brian.dec@ichotelsgroup.com
Sheraton Universal Hotel Universal City, Hollywood California, Wolf Walther, General Manager,
Danise Gembala, Executive Assistant, 1-818-980-1212 or 1-800-325-3535
Six Continents Hotels, Kris Krundwell, www.6c.com 416-675-1342
The Warwick, New York, 54th Street and 6th Avenue 212-247-2700

Other Great Services

Job Placement Specialist, Cathy Zammit, 416-489-3900 ext. 23
Vintage Car Shows, Nick Zammit, 905-392-0780
Jez Enterprises Ltd., Sales, Repairs, Installation of Office Furniture,
John Zarifopoulos 905-279-4180
Wiggins Mechanical Plumbing, Heating and Air Conditioning Services, Alex Schrempf
www.wigginsmechanical.com 416-233-5562
Patti Prest, Murals and Faux Finishes 416-233-8327
Katlin Lowy, Landscape Artist 416-526-7338
www.lkfstudio.com katlin.lowy@sympatico.ca
CleanTech Car Cleaning and Fine Detailing, Jayce King, President 905-453-2002
Pro Look Sweater Cresting and Embroidery, Bob Craig 905-877-8415
The Barbers Chair, Nick 905-820-9960
Anthony, Hairstylist and Colour Specialist: 416-316-9601

Web Design and IT

InterStrata, Victoria Bomben, Frank Fusca, www.intersrata.com. 905-816-1166
Som Phouangpraseuth, IT Consultant ouths@yahoo.ca
The Learning Library, Sabine Steinbrecher, CDO/Founder, 416-703-8674
www.learninglibrary.com
Vision Systems Corp., Michael Curtis 888-578-3247
www.visionsystemscorp.com or info@visionsystems.com
Ingrid Hwan, IT Consultant ingridhwan@hotmail.com
Donna Desormeaux, Positive Marketing Solutions, top2@look.ca 905-821-9454
Steve Carlson, Marketing Options Inc. Planning and Communications Specialist
www.marketingoptions.com or scarlson@pipcom.com 416-690-2662
Codekko Inc., Andre Angel, President and CEO 1-214-561-8664
andreangel@codekko.com

Personal Coaching, Consulting and More

Dan Bodanis Seminars, Workshops, One on One Sales Coaching 905-609-2515
www.danbodanis.com
Dr. Brent Willock, PhD, Psychologist, Psychotherapist, 416-923-5252
Covenant Group, Norm Trainor, CEO 1-877-903-3878
www.covenantgroup.com, or info@covenantgroup.com
Georgian Bay NLP Centre, Deanna Sager, 1-800-279-1757
(Canada & USA) gbnlp@gb-nlp.com
Sara Fernald, www.fernauld.net 705-742-9480
John Kanary International, www.johnkanary.com or jkanary@johnkanary.com
Achieveglobal, Daniel Dea, daniel.dea@achieveglobal.com 416-214-2022
Renton & Associates, Bruce Renton, bruce.renton@sympatico.ca
Workplace Unity, David Roarke, Trauma Therapist, 1-888-834-7073
Program Consultant, droarke@workplaceunity.com

Self Development Courses

Dale Carnegie www.dalecarnegie.com
Mrs. Kathie Mather, President, Dale Carnegie Business Group, 2121 Argentia Road, Suite #103 Mississauga, Ontario L5N-2X4 Canada Phone: 905-826-7300
Fax: 905/826-5565 Email: kathie_mather@dalecarnegie.com
www.ontario.dalecarnegie.com

Zig Ziglar www.zigziglar.com
Tom Hopkins www.tomhopkins.com
Anthony Robbins www.anthonyrobbins.com
Brian Tracy www.briantracy.com
Steven Covey www.stevencovey.com
Jack Canfield www.jackcanfield.com
Mark Victor Hansen www.markvictorhansen.com
Joe Calloway, www.joecalloway.com 1-615-242-4900
Canadian Professional Sales Association www.cpsa.com 145
Wellington St. W., Ste. 610, Toronto, ON M5J 1H8 1-888-267-CPSA
In Toronto (416) 408-2685
American Seminar Leaders Association, info@asla.com 1-800-801-1886
The Strategic Coach, www.strategiccoach.com 1-800-387-3206
www.referralcoach.com Bill Cates Referral Coach International Info@ReferralCoach.com
Toll Free: 800-488-5464 Phone: 301-949-6789 — Fax: 301-949-8564
2915 Fenimore Road, Silver Spring, MD 20902-2600
www.bobburg.com Endless Referrals Burg Communications, Inc.
PO Box 7002 Jupiter, FL 33468-7002 (800) 726-3667 (book) Endless Referrals

Referral Websites, Books, Recordings, Courses, and More!

Rewarding Referrals www.rewardingreferrals.com
Talking Book World Audiobooks, 905-281-2707
mississauga@talkingbooks.com or www.talkingbookworld.com
BNI (Business Network International) www.bnicanada.com, www.bni.com

Available at www.bni.com:

It's In The Cards (book), Dr.Ivan Misener, Candace Bailly, & Dan Georgevich.
Masters of Networking (book), Dr. Ivan Misener, & Don Morgan
The World's Best Known Marketing Secret (book), Dr. Ivan Misener
Business By Referral (book), Dr Ivan Misener, & Robert Davies
Seven Second Marketing (book), by Dr. Ivan Misener

Available at www.amazon.com:

76 Ways to Build a Straight Referral Business, by Lorna Riley CSP
The Secrets of Word of Mouth Marketing: How to Trigger Exponential Sales through Runaway Word of Mouth, by George Silverman
Dig Your Well Before You're Thirsty: The Only Networking Book You'll Ever Need, by Harvey Mackay
The Cycle of Self Empowerment, by Dom Famularo, www.domfamularo.com
The Dynamic Laws of Prosperity, by Catherine Ponder
Leadership Jazz, by Max Depree
Working Women's Art of War, by Chin-Ning Chu
Law of Success, by Napoleon Hill
Think and Grow Rich, by Napoleon Hill
How to Win Friends and Influence People, by Dale Carnegie
How to Stop Worrying and Start Living, by Dale Carnegie
Introducing NLP, Joseph O'Connor and John Seymour
Any book written by the Author Thich Nhat Hanh
Becoming a Category of One, by Joe Calloway